CHARIYA KHATTIYOT
LANNA
RECIPES FROM NORTHERN THAILAND & BEYOND

PHOTOGRAPHY BY CLARE WINFIELD

RYLAND PETERS & SMALL

Senior Designer Megan Smith
Senior Editor Abi Waters
Editorial Director Julia Charles
Production Manager Gordana Simakovic
Creative Director Leslie Harrington
Food Stylist Jennifer Joyce
Prop Stylist Rosie Jenkins
Indexer Vanessa Bird

First published in 2025 by
Ryland Peters & Small
20–21 Jockey's Fields,
London WC1R 4BW
and
1452 Davis Bugg Road
Warrenton, NC 27589

www.rylandpeters.com
email: euregulations@rylandpeters.com

10 9 8 7 6 5 4 3 2 1

Text © Chariya Khattiyot 2025
Design and photography
© Ryland Peters & Small 2025

Printed in China.

The author's moral rights have been asserted. All rights reserved. No part of this publication may be reproduced, stored in a retrieval system or transmitted in any form or by any means, electronic, mechanical, photocopying or otherwise, without the prior permission of the publisher.

ISBN: 978-1-78879-714-6

A CIP record for this book is available from the British Library. US Library of Congress cataloging-in-Publication Data has been applied for.

The authorised representative in the EEA is Authorised Rep Compliance Ltd., Ground Floor, 71 Lower Baggot Street, Dublin, D02 P593, Ireland
www.arccompliance.com

NOTES
• Butter is always unsalted, unless specified otherwise.
• Eggs are always UK large/US extra-large.
• Herbs are always fresh, unless specified otherwise.
• All vegetables are peeled, unless specified otherwise.
• When a recipe calls for the grated zest of citrus fruit, use unwaxed fruit and wash well before using.
• Both metric and imperial measurements are used in the recipes. Follow one set of measurements throughout as they are not necessarily interchangeable.
• All spoon measurements are level, unless specified otherwise.
5 ml = 1 teaspoon
15 ml = 1 tablespoon
• Ovens should be preheated to the specified temperature.
• Uncooked or partially cooked eggs should not be served to the very old, frail, young children, pregnant women or those with compromised immune systems.

Contents

The vibrant world of Thai cuisine 6

1. **Street food** 14
2. **Salads & appetizers** 42
3. **Soups & broths** 68
4. **Curries** 92
5. **Stir-fries** 112
6. **Traditional dishes** 130
7. **Sweet things** 154

Index 174

Acknowledgements 176

The vibrant world of THAI CUISINE

I grew up in Northern Thailand, surrounded by beautiful landscapes, fresh ingredients and warm-hearted people. Since I was young, I have loved cooking. I spent my childhood watching my family prepare meals with so much care and love, using herbs and spices picked straight from the garden. The way they balanced flavours and turned simple ingredients into something special fascinated me.

From the busy street markets of Chiang Mai to small village kitchens, I learned the secrets of Northern Thai food – where fresh herbs, fragrant spices and rich flavours make every dish special. Northern Thai cuisine is all about depth and balance. The warmth of turmeric, the earthiness of coriander/cilantro, the heat of chillies/chiles, and the creaminess of coconut milk all come together to create dishes that are bold yet comforting. These recipes have been passed down for generations, keeping our culture and traditions alive.

Food is more than just something to eat – it is a way of bringing people together. In my family, cooking was not just about feeding ourselves, but about sharing joy, love and memories. Sitting down to eat a meal was a time for laughter, storytelling and connection. That is what I want to share with you in this book – not just recipes, but a piece of my heart and the culture that shaped me.

As I continued my journey, I became curious about food from other places. I started exploring different cuisines, tasting new flavours and learning how people cook around the world. Every new dish I tried taught me something, and I realized that food is a universal language. It brings people together, no matter where they are from. This inspired me to create my own unique dishes. This book brings together my favourite recipes from Northern Thailand, along with special dishes from other regions. Whether you are looking for a comforting bowl of Northern Thai curry, a refreshing herbal salad or a spicy stir-fry that wakes up your taste buds, there is something for everyone.

DIVERSITY AROUND THE COUNTRY

Thailand's cuisine is incredibly diverse, and each region has its own special flavours:

NORTHERN THAI – dishes are rich and aromatic, with influences from Burma and Laos. They often use turmeric, lemongrass and coconut milk to create comforting, flavourful curries and soups.

NORTHEASTERN THAI – (Isaan cuisine) is bold and spicy, with dishes like *som tam* (swede salad) and *larb gai* (spicy minced meat) that are full of fresh herbs and tangy lime.

CENTRAL THAI – offers a balance of sweet, sour, salty and spicy flavours. It includes famous dishes like *pad Thai*, *tom yum* and green curry – some of the most well-loved Thai foods around the world.

SOUTHERN THAI – known for its fiery heat and intense flavours, with curries that are deep, rich and often made with seafood and coconut (i.e. jungle curry).

COOKING SHOULD BE FUN AND EASY

It doesn't matter if you are an experienced cook or just starting out – this book will help you feel confident in the kitchen. I have kept the recipes simple, with easy-to-follow instructions and helpful tips. You don't need hard-to-find ingredients or fancy equipment. Many of the dishes can be made with ingredients from your local supermarket, and I will also share ways to substitute things if needed.

I share stories and memories connected to these dishes. Whether it's a dish I grew up eating with my family or one that reminds me of my travels, I want you to feel the love and culture behind every bite.

One of the most important things I learned from cooking is that food is meant to be shared. Whether you are making a quick meal for yourself or preparing a feast for friends and family, I hope this book inspires you to enjoy the process, experiment with flavours and have fun in the kitchen.

Thai ingredients
The heart of Thai cooking

Thailand is a beautiful country with rich soil, clean water and a tropical climate, making it a perfect place for growing a variety of fresh ingredients. Thai cuisine is famous for bold flavours, vibrant colours and fragrant aromas, and much of this comes from the high-quality, natural ingredients available all year round.

Some ingredients are staples in every Thai household, found in almost every dish. These include dried chillies/chiles, shrimp paste, fish sauce and fermented fish. These core ingredients form the foundation of Thai cooking, bringing the deep, complex and umami-rich flavours that make Thai food so unique.

When I was growing up, we didn't have a lot of money to buy food from the markets every day. Instead, we relied on what we could grow in our garden. Our home was surrounded by fruit trees, vegetables and herbs, which became a part of our daily meals. We would go outside in the morning and pick whatever was available, turning simple ingredients into flavourful dishes.

We would make curries with wild vegetables, stir-fries with fresh herbs and even snacks using fruits from the trees. For example, young jackfruit was often used to make a hearty curry, while banana blossoms could be turned into a delicious salad. Even banana leaves had a purpose – they were used to wrap food for steaming or grilling. Nothing went to waste!

As long as we had our staple ingredients we could always create something delicious without spending extra money. Even now, I still keep these essential ingredients in my cupboard because they remind me of home.

ESSENTIAL THAI INGREDIENTS

If you want to cook authentic Thai food, there are some key ingredients you should try to keep in your kitchen. However, I understand that not everyone has access to traditional Thai ingredients. That's why, in this book, I've included alternatives that you can use in place of harder-to-find items. While the taste may not be exactly the same, these substitutes will still allow you to enjoy delicious, Thai-inspired dishes at home.

Thai cooking is all about balancing flavours – sweet, salty, sour, spicy and umami. So even if you need to substitute some ingredients, as long as you achieve this balance, your dish will still taste amazing!

FRESH

MAKRUT LIME LEAVES (*Bai makrut* ใบมะกรูด)
These fragrant leaves provide a unique citrusy aroma. Often used in *tom yum* soup, curries and stir-fries.
Alternative if lime leaves are hard to find, try using grated lime zest for a similar fresh citrus flavour.

LEMONGRASS (*Ta khrai* ตะไคร้)
Lemongrass adds a fresh, citrusy fragrance to many Thai dishes, especially soups, curries and marinades.
Alternative A mix of lemon zest and fresh ginger can give a similar flavour if fresh lemongrass is unavailable.

GALANGAL (*Kha* ข่า)
Galangal is a root similar to fresh ginger but has a more citrusy, peppery taste. It is an essential ingredient in *tom kha gai* (coconut chicken soup).
Alternative If you can't find fresh galangal, you can use fresh ginger, but the taste will be slightly different.

THAI BASIL (*Bai horapa* ใบโหระพา)
This has a lightly spicy, anise flavour and is commonly used in stir-fried dishes like Thai basil chicken.
Alternative Regular or Italian basil can be used.

CORIANDER/CILANTRO (*Pak chi* ผักชี)
Both the leaves and stalks are used in Thai cooking. The leaves add a citrusy, herby note to curries and soups, while the stalks are a key base for marinades and spice pastes.

LIMES (*Ma now* มะนาว)
A signature Thai ingredient that provides acidity and brightness. Used in soups like *tom yum*, salads like *som tam* and as a finishing touch for grilled meat and seafood dishes.

PANTRY

FISH SAUCE (*Nam pla* น้ำปลา)
Fish sauce is one of the most important seasonings in Thai cuisine. It adds a deep, salty and slightly sweet umami flavour to dishes. Made from fermented fish, it is used in everything from stir-fries to soups and dipping sauces.
Alternative If you can't find fish sauce, you can use soy sauce or a mix of soy sauce and a little anchovy paste for a similar umami taste.

DRIED CHILLIES/CHILES (*Prik haeng* พริกแห้ง)
Thai cuisine is known for its spicy and bold flavours, and dried chillies are a big part of that. They are used in curry pastes, stir-fries and chilli sauces. I often use a mix of different sized dried chillies in my chilli pastes to get the right balance of colour and heat. The large dried red chillies are used to provide colour and the medium or small dried red chillies provide the heat. Feel free to alter the amounts or balance of sizes according to your heat preferences though.
Alternative Cayenne pepper or dried chilli/hot red pepper flakes can be used as a substitute.

SHRIMP PASTE (*Kapi* กะปิ)
Shrimp paste is a strong, pungent ingredient made from fermented ground shrimp. It is used in Thai curries, chili pastes and even some stir-fried dishes. Using shrimp paste is really up to your own preference – if you're not a fan, feel free to reduce the amount suggested in recipes.
Alternative If shrimp paste is unavailable, try using miso paste with a little fish sauce for depth of flavour.

COCONUT MILK (*Gati* กะทิ)
Coconut milk is essential for creamy curries like *khao soi*, green curry and massaman curry. It adds richness and balances the heat from spices.
Alternative If fresh coconut milk is unavailable, canned coconut milk works well. For a lighter version, use coconut water mixed with a little coconut cream.

RICE NOODLES (*Sen khao* เส้นขาว)
Made from rice flour, these come in various thicknesses, from thin (*sen mee*) to wide (*sen yai*), commonly used in pad Thai, pad kee mow and soups.

EGG NOODLES (*Ba mee* บะหมี่)
Made from wheat flour and egg, they have a chewy texture. Often used in stir-fries or noodle soups.

LIGHT SOY SAUCE (*See ew khao* ซีอิ๊วขาว)
Salty and slightly sweet, used in stir-fries and marinades.

DARK SOY SAUCE (*See ew dam* ซีอิ๊วดำ)
Thicker, richer and slightly sweet, and used for colour and depth in dishes.

TAMARIND (*Ma kham* มะขาม)
A sour fruit used in paste form to add a tangy-sweet depth to Thai dishes like pad Thai, curries and dipping sauces. It balances flavours beautifully in Thai cooking.

PEANUTS (*Tua lisong* ถั่วลิสง)
A key ingredient in Thai cuisine, often roasted and crushed for dishes like pad Thai, swede salad and curries. Adds nuttiness, crunch and richness.

CREATING A THAI BANQUET

A Thai banquet is a feast of flavours, textures and colours, designed for sharing. All dishes are served at once, creating a harmonious balance of sweet, sour, salty and spicy flavours. A typical Thai banquet includes curries, stir-fries, grilled or fried delights, salads, soups and rice. It isn't just about food, it's about togetherness, with dishes enjoyed in a lively, communal setting.

Street food
อาหารสตรีทฟู้ด

A symphony of spices
and textures that celebrates
the best of Thai cuisine.

MOO PING

Grilled pork skewer

Moo Ping is my go-to dish whenever I have the time to fire up a charcoal barbecue (although, these skewers are equally good when cooked in a pan or on a griddle). The aroma of the charcoal and smoke instantly takes me back to the street-food stalls in Thailand. This dish offers a delightful mix of sweet and savoury flavours, perfectly complemented by a spicy and tangy dipping sauce. Back in my university days, there was a *Moo Ping* stall near my dorm, and I made it a daily treat!

4 garlic cloves, crushed/minced
½ teaspoon coriander seeds
½ teaspoon ground white pepper
small handful chopped coriander/cilantro stalks (no leaves)
500 g/1 lb 2 oz. pork collar or shoulder steaks, thinly sliced
4 tablespoons brown sugar
1 tablespoon fish sauce
1 makrut lime leaf, finely chopped
1 tablespoon cornflour/cornstarch
1 tablespoon dark soy sauce
1 tablespoon oyster sauce
2 tablespoons vegetable oil, plus extra for frying
150 g/⅔ cup coconut milk
sticky or boiled rice, to serve (optional)

DIPPING SAUCE
2 large red chillies/chiles, chopped
3 garlic cloves, crushed/minced
3 tablespoons brown sugar
4 tablespoons fish sauce
4 tablespoons lime juice
6 tablespoons hot water
3–4 sprigs of coriander/cilantro, leaves finely chopped

6–8 bamboo skewers, soaked in warm water for 30 minutes

SERVES 2–3

In a mortar and pestle, pound the garlic, coriander seeds, white pepper and coriander stalks to a smooth paste.

In a mixing bowl, combine the pork with the paste, then add the brown sugar, fish sauce, lime leaf, cornflour, dark soy sauce, oyster sauce, vegetable oil and coconut milk. Mix it until well combined. Keep it in the fridge for 1 hour to marinate.

Thread the marinated pork onto the soaked bamboo skewers.

Heat a frying pan/skillet over a high heat and brush the pan with a little vegetable oil to prevent sticking. Place the skewers in the pan and cook for 3–4 minutes on each side, turning them occasionally to ensure they are evenly cooked.

Meanwhile, make the sauce. In a small food processor, blend the large red chillies and garlic. Transfer to a bowl and add the brown sugar, fish sauce, lime juice and hot water, then add the chopped coriander and mix well until the sugar is dissolved.

Once cooked, remove the skewers from the pan and serve with the dipping sauce and either sticky rice or boiled rice, as you prefer.

TOD MUN PLA

Thai fish cakes

This recipe brings back memories of my first big cooking project at school. We had to set up a food stall for one day as part of a school event, so my friends and I decided to make *Tod Mun Pla*. Back then, there was no internet, so we all went to the library to find a recipe.

Over the years, I've made this dish countless times, experimenting with different types of fish and tweaking recipes along the way. After much trial and error, I've perfected a recipe that I'm proud of – it's the one I use at my restaurant. *Tod Mun Pla* has become a popular starter on the menu, loved for its bold flavours and crispy texture.

500 g/1 lb 2 oz. frozen basa fillets (or any other frozen white fish), defrosted and chopped
10 dried red chillies/chiles, ground
1 teaspoon shrimp paste (optional)
3 garlic cloves, crushed/minced
1 small shallot, crushed/minced
100 g/3½ oz. frozen king prawns/ jumbo shrimp, peeled and deveined (do not defrost)
1 egg
1 tablespoon tapioca starch (or cornflour/cornstarch)
1 tablespoon paprika
1 tablespoon fish sauce (increase to 2 tablespoons if not using shrimp paste)
1 teaspoon palm sugar (or brown sugar)
1 teaspoon salt
100 g/3½ oz. fine green beans, finely chopped
3 makrut lime leaves, finely chopped (or use the grated zest of ½ lime)
3 sprigs of coriander/cilantro, finely chopped, plus extra to garnish
500 ml/2 cups vegetable oil
chopped red chilli/chile, to garnish
sweet chilli sauce, to serve

SERVES 4

In a food processor, combine half of the fish fillets with the ground chillies, shrimp paste (if using), garlic and shallot. Blend until smooth, ensuring no large chunks remain.

Add the frozen king prawns (keeping them frozen helps maintain the batter's cold temperature), the rest of the fish, the egg, tapioca starch, paprika, fish sauce, sugar and salt. Blend until well combined.

Transfer the batter to a mixing bowl and gently fold in the finely chopped green beans, lime leaves and coriander until evenly mixed.

Heat the vegetable oil in a large frying pan/skillet over a medium-high heat. Scoop up some of the fish cake batter (about a heaped tablespoon) and carefully drop it into the hot oil. Press it down with the back of a spoon to make a patty (with a diameter of about 5–6 cm/2–2½ inches). Fry for about 2 minutes, then flip over and cook on the other side for a further 2 minutes, or until golden brown. Remove the fish cakes and let them rest on paper towels to drain any excess oil. Cook one batch at a time, just enough to fill the pan. How many you can cook in a batch depends on the size of your pan and how big you make the fish cakes. Repeat until all the batter is used.

To serve, arrange the fish cakes on a plate and garnish with chopped coriander and chilli. Serve with sweet chilli sauce for dipping.

ขนมจีนน้ำยา
KANOM JEEN NAM YA

Rice noodles with fish curry sauce

This is a famous Thai dish commonly found in markets and at street-food stalls throughout Thailand. It features rice noodles served with a creamy fish curry sauce made from a blend of spices, fresh herbs and coconut milk. Traditionally, freshwater fatty fish is used, but in this recipe, canned tuna is used for convenience – it's easy to find and still delicious.

5 large red chillies/chiles, chopped
2 teaspoons hot chilli powder
2 stalks of Chinese key root (or a thumb-sized piece of fresh ginger), finely chopped
3 garlic cloves, finely chopped
1 small shallot, finely chopped
1 lemongrass stalk, finely chopped
1 teaspoon shrimp paste (optional)
2 tablespoons sunflower or vegetable oil
400 ml/14 fl oz. coconut milk (at least 65% fat content)
3 tablespoons fish sauce
3 teaspoons palm sugar (or brown sugar)
200 g/7 oz. canned tuna, drained
150 g/5½ oz. vermicelli rice noodles

GARNISH
handful of beansprouts
small handful of fine green beans, finely chopped
sprig of coriander/cilantro, finely chopped
1 spring onion/scallion, finely chopped
1 sprig of Thai basil, leaves picked (optional)
1 red chilli/chile, chopped
lime wedges, for squeezing

SERVES 2

Place the red chillies in a medium-size jug/pitcher, along with the hot chilli powder, Chinese key root (or fresh ginger), garlic, shallot, lemongrass and shrimp paste (if using). Use a handheld blender to blend to a smooth paste, adding some water as needed to help loosen the mixture.

Heat the oil in a saucepan over a medium heat. Add the blended chilli paste and cook for 2–3 minutes until fragrant.

Add the coconut milk and stir through. Season with fish sauce and palm sugar, then add the drained tuna and simmer for 10 minutes.

Bring a small saucepan of water to the boil, then add the vermicelli rice noodles (making sure the noodles are fully submerged). Cook the noodles for 2–3 minutes, then drain and drizzle with a little of the cooking oil to prevent sticking.

Place the cooked noodles in a deep bowl, top with the curry, then arrange some beansprouts and fine green beans on top. Sprinkle with coriander, spring onion, Thai basil (if using), sliced red chilli and lime wedges on the side for squeezing over.

COOKING TIP There are many coconut milk brands available, but I've found that those with 65% or higher fat content work best. They have a richer, creamier consistency, and are less watery, making them perfect for these types of recipes.

KHAO MUN GAI

Hainanese chicken rice

Khao Mun Gai will always hold a special place in my heart because it was my brother's favourite dish. The tender chicken, fragrant rice and tangy dipping sauce always brought a big smile to his face, especially when he could have extra sauce. Cooking it now fills me with bittersweet joy; it's a way to remember him and the bond we shared, as if he's still here, enjoying his favourite meal with me.

3 tablespoons vegetable oil
thumb-sized piece of fresh ginger, sliced
4 garlic cloves, bruised
500 g/1 lb 2 oz. jasmine rice
650 ml/2⅔ cups chicken stock (see below)
2 tablespoons light soy sauce

CHICKEN STOCK
1 kg/2¼ lb. chicken thighs (bones can be removed or left in according to your preference)
10 g/⅓ oz. salt
2 chicken stock cubes
4 garlic cloves, bruised
3 sprigs of coriander/cilantro

DIPPING SAUCE
3 tablespoons light soy sauce
3 tablespoons brown sugar
5 tablespoons hot water
1 tablespoon soy bean paste (or white miso paste)
3 tablespoons lime juice
3 garlic cloves, crushed/minced
2 large red chillies/chiles, finely chopped
thumb-sized piece of fresh ginger, crushed/minced
3 sprigs of coriander/cilantro, chopped

GARNISH
chopped coriander/cilantro leaves
1 cucumber, halved and sliced lengthways

SERVES 3–4

First, make the chicken stock. Place the chicken thighs in a saucepan and add 1.5 litres/6 cups water, the salt, chicken stock cubes, garlic and coriander. Bring the water to a gentle simmer, cover and cook for 15 minutes over a medium heat. Remove the chicken and set aside, keeping the broth in the pan.

In a separate pan, heat the vegetable oil. Sauté the ginger and garlic until golden and fragrant. Add the jasmine rice and stir until all the grains are coated. Pour in the stock from the pan you cooked the chicken in earlier, then add the light soy sauce.

Nestle the partially cooked chicken thighs back into the pan with the rice. Cover and cook over a low heat for 15–20 minutes until the rice is tender and the chicken is fully cooked.

Meanwhile, make the dipping sauce. Combine the soy sauce, brown sugar, hot water, soy bean paste, lime juice, garlic, red chillies, ginger and coriander in a bowl. Stir until mixed thoroughly. Adjust the seasoning to taste, balancing the sweet, sour, salty and spicy flavours.

Remove the chicken thighs from the pan and slice into bite-sized pieces. Scoop out and discard the whole garlic cloves and any ginger slices you can find.

Serve the chicken over the fragrant rice with small bowls of the dipping sauce and broth from the pan on the side. Garnish the chicken and rice with cucumber slices and sprigs of coriander.

ไก่สะเต๊ะ
GAI SATAY

Chicken satay

Chicken satay is a popular street-food dish in Thailand. It features chicken skewers grilled and served with a creamy, slightly sweet peanut dipping sauce. The chicken is marinated in a blend of spices, coconut milk and turmeric, giving it a rich, aromatic flavour.

1 teaspoon curry powder
1 teaspoon hot chilli powder
¼ teaspoon ground turmeric
4 tablespoons coconut milk
1 teaspoon palm sugar
  (or brown sugar)
1 tablespoon fish sauce
400 g/14 oz. boneless and skinless chicken thighs, sliced into 2.5-cm/1-inch pieces

SATAY SAUCE
2 tablespoons vegetable oil
2 garlic cloves, crushed/minced
1 tablespoon hot chilli powder
400 ml/14 fl oz. coconut milk (at least 65% fat content so it's not too watery)
2 tablespoons peanut butter (smooth or crunchy)
2 tablespoons fish sauce
4 tablespoons palm sugar (or brown sugar)
grated zest of 1 lime
4 tablespoons lime juice
2 sprigs of coriander/cilantro, finely chopped

4–6 bamboo skewers, soaked in warm water for 30 minutes

SERVES 2–3
(MAKES 4–6 SKEWERS)

Combine the curry powder, hot chilli powder, turmeric, coconut milk, palm sugar and fish sauce in a large mixing bowl. Add the chicken and mix to coat in the marinade. Cover with cling film/plastic wrap and refrigerate for at least 30 minutes, or until ready to use (but best left overnight to marinade).

To make the satay sauce, heat the vegetable oil in a saucepan over a medium heat, then add the garlic and chilli powder. Stir for 1 minute to release the flavours.

Add the coconut milk, peanut butter, fish sauce, palm sugar, lime zest and lime juice. Cook over a medium heat, stirring continuously, until well combined, then lower the heat and simmer for a further 2–3 minutes. Adjust the seasoning to taste, balancing the sweet, sour, salty and spicy flavours, then add the chopped coriander and set aside (the sauce could be made up to a week in advance and kept in the fridge).

Thread 3–4 pieces of marinated chicken onto each skewer.

Heat a frying pan/skillet over a medium-high heat and brush with a little vegetable oil. Cook the skewers for around 3–4 minutes on each side until the chicken is cooked through and slightly charred.

Coat the chicken with some of the satay sauce you made earlier. Serve the skewers with some extra satay sauce on the side for dipping and a few fresh vegetables like baby gem lettuce and cucumber, if liked.

COOKING TIPS If you are using coconut milk with a fat content of less than 65%, which has the consistency of milk rather than cream, you may need to reduce the amount in the satay sauce. Start with 200 ml (7 fl oz.), then add more to achieve the consistency of sauce you prefer.

I used a frying pan to cook these skewers on the hob/stovetop, but you can use any hot griddle pan, or you can cook them under a grill/broiler or bake them in the oven – whatever is easiest for you at home.

ยำทะเล
YAM TALAY

Mixed seafood salad

Yam Talay reminds me of a school trip to Pattaya, in the south of Thailand. Back home in the north, we don't eat much seafood because it's hard to transport, and we didn't have good refrigerators back then. But in Pattaya, seafood is everywhere! It was my first time trying *Yam Talay*, full of fresh prawns, squid and mussels, mixed with lime and chilli. It tasted so fresh and spicy, so different from what I was used to. I still think about that trip every time I eat *Yam Talay*!

100 g/3½ oz. glass noodles
100 g/3½ oz. king prawns/jumbo shrimp, peeled and deveined
100 g/3½ oz. squid, sliced
100 g/3½ oz. mussel meat
100 g/3½ oz. seafood sticks, sliced
1 small carrot, shredded
50 g/1¾ oz. fennel, thinly sliced
5–6 small pickled onions, halved and drained (but keep the juice)
10 cherry tomatoes, halved
1 red onion, thinly sliced
small handful of coriander/cilantro, chopped, plus extra to garnish
4 spring onions/scallions, chopped

DRESSING
2 large hot red chillies/chiles, finely chopped, plus extra to garnish
4 tablespoons fish sauce
3 tablespoons lime juice
1 tablespoon brown sugar
2 tablespoons pickle juice (from the pickled onions above)
3 garlic cloves, crushed/minced

SERVES 2

Soak the glass noodles in warm water for 15–20 minutes until softened. Drain and set aside.

Bring a saucepan of water to the boil. Add the prawns, squid, mussels and seafood sticks. Cook for 2–3 minutes until just cooked through. Drain and set aside.

To make the dressing, in a mixing bowl, combine the chillies, fish sauce, lime juice, brown sugar, pickle juice and garlic, stirring until the sugar dissolves. Adjust the seasoning to taste, balancing the sweet, sour, salty and spicy flavours.

In a large bowl, mix the cooked seafood, softened glass noodles, carrot, fennel, pickled onions, tomatoes, red onion, coriander and spring onions.

Pour the dressing over the salad. Gently toss everything together until the dressing coats all the ingredients. Transfer to a serving plate and garnish with extra coriander or chilli, if desired.

HOY TOD
หอยทอด

Thai-style mussel pancakes

Hoy Tod is a well-known Thai street-food dish, but I have to admit I wasn't a fan at first. I never really liked oysters, which is the traditional way it's made. Later on, I discovered that it can be made with mussels instead – and since I love mussels, I decided to create my own version of the dish.

I initially experimented with this recipe while spending a summer in Ireland. My other half's family home is near the seaside, and we visit every summer. It's a quiet, small village, far from tourist spots, and one of my favourite things to do there is foraging for cockles and mussels along the shore. I still remember finding mussels hidden under the seaweed on the big rocks near the water. There were hundreds of them, both small and large. We made sure to leave the little ones behind and only picked the big ones. The freshness of those mussels, straight from the sea, made the dish even more special.

120 g/1 cup self-raising/rising flour
40 g/3 tablespoons rice flour
40 g/3 tablespoons cornflour/cornstarch
10 g/2 teaspoons baking powder
pinch each of salt and freshly ground black pepper
250 ml/1 cup ice-cold water
1 tablespoon light soy sauce
2 teaspoons brown sugar
3 large/US extra-large eggs (about 180 g/6 oz.)
small handful of chives, chopped
300 g/10½ oz. mussel meat
4 tablespoons vegetable oil, for frying

DIPPING SAUCE
100 g/scant ½ cup tomato ketchup
3½ tablespoons tamarind paste
100 g/scant ½ cup sriracha or other hot sauce
50 g/¼ cup brown sugar

GARNISH
100 g/3½ oz. beansprouts
chopped coriander/cilantro leaves

SERVES 2–3

In a mixing bowl, combine the self-raising flour, rice flour, cornflour, baking powder, salt and pepper. Slowly pour in the ice-cold water while stirring until you get a smooth batter. Add the soy sauce and sugar and mix well.

Crack the eggs into the batter and stir until combined. Fold in the chopped chives and mussel meat.

Heat a non-stick pan over a medium-high heat and add a generous amount of oil. Pour a ladle of the batter into the pan, spreading it evenly, and cook until crispy on the edges and golden brown underneath. Flip and cook the other side until crispy and cooked through. Repeat until all the batter is used.

To make the dipping sauce, mix the ketchup, tamarind paste, hot sauce and brown sugar in a small bowl until well combined.

Serve the pancakes hot, folded in half or into quarters, topped with fresh beansprouts and chopped coriander, with the dipping sauce on the side.

KAI TOD PU

Chunky crab omelette
with spicy fish sauce

This is a dish I created a few years ago after hearing about a street-food stall in Bangkok that received a Michelin star. The dish that won the award was this simple yet luxurious crab omelette, and I was instantly inspired to try it at home. I recreated it using ingredients that are easier to find here in England, while still capturing the rich, fluffy texture of the omelette and the bold flavours of the spicy fish sauce. It's a tribute to the original dish and proof that even the simplest street food can become something extraordinary.

100 g/3½ oz. canned chunky crab meat, drained
3 large/US extra-large eggs, beaten
50 g/scant ¼ cup evaporated milk
1 tablespoon light soy sauce
½ teaspoon ground white pepper
200 ml/scant 1 cup vegetable oil, for frying

DIPPING SAUCE
2 birds eye chillies/chiles, finely chopped
2 garlic cloves, crushed/minced
1 small shallot, finely chopped
100 ml/scant ½ cup fish sauce

GARNISH
1 large red chilli/chile, sliced
chopped coriander/cilantro leaves

SERVES 1–2

In a bowl, combine the crab meat, beaten eggs, evaporated milk, soy sauce and white pepper. Mix gently to avoid breaking up the crab meat too much.

Heat the vegetable oil in a deep frying pan/skillet or wok over a medium-high heat. Once the oil is hot, carefully pour the egg mixture into the pan. Cook for 2–3 minutes on each side, spooning hot oil over the top to help it puff up and cook evenly.

Once golden brown and set, carefully flip the omelette and cook for a further 2–3 minutes until both sides are golden. Remove from the pan and drain on paper towels to remove any excess oil.

Meanwhile, prepare the dipping sauce. Mix the chillies, garlic, shallot and fish sauce in a small bowl, adjusting the heat levels to taste.

Transfer the omelette to a serving plate, garnish with red chilli and coriander leaves, then serve hot with the dipping sauce on the side.

เบอร์เก้อไก่
ROU JIA MO

Chinese chicken burger
with spicy Asian-style salad

Rou Jia Mo, often called the 'Chinese burger', inspired me to create a version filled with spiced, tender chicken paired with a refreshing Asian-style salad. I developed this dish for a food festival last year using a quick, no-proofing bread with a texture similar to an English muffin. The savoury, slightly sweet chicken filling pairs perfectly with the bread, while the crisp cabbage, carrots and tangy sesame dressing add vibrant, fresh flavours to complete the dish.

DOUGH
- **500 g/3½ cups strong white flour**
- **1 teaspoon salt**
- **1 tablespoon caster/superfine sugar**
- **2 teaspoons baking powder**
- **7 g/¼ oz. instant dried yeast** (normally it comes in 7-g/¼-oz. sachets, or use 1½ teaspoons)
- **280 g/generous 1 cup water**
- **2 tablespoons vegetable oil**

FILLING
- **2 tablespoons vegetable oil**
- **4 garlic cloves, crushed/minced**
- **1 onion, sliced**
- **400 g/14 oz. chicken breast,** thinly sliced
- **2 teaspoons curry powder**
- **½ teaspoon ground turmeric**
- **½ teaspoon ground coriander**
- **½ teaspoon ground cumin**
- **1 teaspoon hot chilli powder**
- **1 tablespoon brown sugar**
- **3 tablespoons light soy sauce**
- **1 tablespoon rice vinegar** (or cider vinegar)
- **3 teaspoons sriracha or other hot sauce**
- **3 tablespoons smooth peanut butter**
- **200 ml/scant 1 cup coconut milk**

SPICY ASIAN-STYLE SALAD
- **200 g/7 oz. red cabbage, shredded**
- **200 g/7 oz. white cabbage, shredded**
- **1 carrot, shredded**
- **100 g/1¾ cup beansprouts**
- **3 spring onions/scallions, chopped**
- **1 large red chilli/chile, thinly sliced**
- **3 sprigs of coriander/cilantro, chopped**
- **10 mint leaves (optional)**

DRESSING
- **3 tablespoons rice vinegar** (or cider vinegar)
- **2 garlic cloves, crushed/minced**
- **1 tablespoon fish sauce**
- **4 tablespoons light soy sauce**
- **3 tablespoons brown sugar**
- **2 tablespoons lime juice**
- **2 tablespoons cider vinegar**
- **3 tablespoons hot water**

MAKES 4–6 BURGERS

First, make the dough. In the bowl of an electric stand mixer, combine the flour, salt, sugar, baking powder and yeast. Gradually add the water and vegetable oil. Knead the dough with the hook attachment on a medium speed for 10–15 minutes until smooth and elastic. Cover the dough with a damp cloth and rest for 10–15 minutes.

Next, prepare the filling. Heat the vegetable oil in a frying pan/skillet over a medium-high heat. Add the garlic, onion and chicken and stir-fry until the chicken is fully cooked. Add all the remaining ingredients for the filling, then adjust the seasoning to taste, balancing the sweet, sour, salty and spicy flavours. Set the filling aside to cool.

To make the salad, in a mixing bowl, combine the shredded cabbage, carrot, beansprouts, spring onions, red chilli, coriander and mint (if using). Toss to mix evenly.

In a separate bowl, combine all the salad dressing ingredients and mix well until fully combined. Pour the dressing over the salad and toss gently, ensuring everything is evenly coated.

Divide the dough into equal portions (you should get about 4–6 pieces, depending on the desired size). Shape each portion into a ball and gently flatten into a disc about 1 cm/½ inch thick.

Heat a non-stick frying pan/skillet over a medium heat and lightly grease it with vegetable oil. Cook each dough disc for 1–2 minutes on each side until lightly golden.

Preheat the oven to 200°C/180°C fan/400°F/Gas 6.

Transfer the pan-fried dough to a baking sheet lined with parchment paper. Bake for 10–12 minutes or until the dough is fully cooked and slightly puffed.

Slice each of the cooked breads in half horizontally to form a bun. Fill each one with the prepared chicken filling and a generous portion of the dressed salad. Garnish with sliced red chilli and coriander leaves. Serve the warm stuffed buns alongside any extra dressed salad.

SALAPAO SAI MOO

Thai steamed buns

Growing up we didn't have much money, so buying *salapao* wasn't something we did often. Every evening, a merchant with a motorcycle trailer would come by. The kids in the neighbourhood would rush out, hoping for one of those soft, fluffy buns filled with sweet and savoury pork. The price of one *salapao* was more than the cost of a whole meal, so we only watched as others enjoyed them. Whenever I make or eat *salapao*, it reminds me of those evenings and how something so simple can feel so special.

DOUGH
360 g/2½ cups strong white flour, plus extra for dusting
20 g/4 teaspoons caster/superfine sugar
7 g/¼ oz. instant dried yeast
1 teaspoon baking powder
80 g/3 oz. milk powder
200 g/scant 1 cup warm water (just a bit too warm to touch, but not boiling)
2 tablespoons vegetable oil

FILLING
250 g/9 oz. minced/ground pork
½ a small carrot, finely chopped
2 spring onions/scallions, finely chopped
1½ tablespoons light soy sauce
1½ tablespoons oyster sauce
½ tablespoon sesame oil
1½ tablespoons honey
½ teaspoon ground white pepper
2 tablespoons cornflour/cornstarch
sweet chilli sauce, to serve

a steamer lined with parchment paper

MAKES 6–8 BUNS

First, make the dough. In a large bowl, combine the flour, sugar, yeast, baking powder and milk powder and mix well. Gradually add the warm water and oil and stir until the dough comes together.

Knead the dough on a lightly floured work surface for 15–20 minutes, or until smooth and elastic. Alternatively, use an electric stand mixer fitted with a dough hook for 7–10 minutes. Cover the dough with cling film/plastic wrap and prove in a warm place for 1 hour, or until doubled in size.

Meanwhile, make the filling. Combine the pork, carrot and spring onions in a bowl. Add the soy sauce, oyster sauce, sesame oil, honey, white pepper and cornflour. Mix, cover and refrigerate until needed.

Once the dough has risen, punch it down to release any air bubbles and knead briefly. Divide the dough into 6–8 equal pieces. Roll each piece into a ball, then flatten it into a disc. Divide the filling evenly between the discs, placing it in the centre. Gather the edges of the dough over the filling and tightly pinch them together to seal the bun and prevent leaking. Place each bun on squares of parchment paper and leave them to proof for 20–30 minutes until slightly puffy.

Place a steamer over a medium heat. Once the water is boiling, add the buns, leaving enough space between each one for them to expand. Steam for 20–25 minutes, or until the dough is fluffy and the filling is cooked. Carefully remove the buns from the steamer and let them cool for a few minutes. Serve while still warm with sweet chilli sauce.

COOKING TIP To speed up the proving process, place a glass of water in the microwave and heat for 1 minute. Remove the water, place the covered dough in the microwave (turned off) and leave it to proof for 15 minutes. The warm, moist environment significantly reduces the proving time.

ปีกไก่ทอดกระเทียม
PEEK GAI TOD KRATIAM

Crispy garlic chicken wings

Peek Gai Tod Kratiam brings back warm memories of my childhood summers in Thailand. Every summer holiday, my mum would set up a small food stall in front of our house just for me. I'd sell these chicken wings to locals passing by. The crispy, garlicky chicken pairs perfectly with the fresh and spicy swede salad on page 47; it's ideal food for a hot Thai summer. Many customers enjoyed their snack with a cold beer, and I couldn't blame them. Good food and a cold drink on a hot day feels like pure heaven. Those summers taught me how food brings people together on joyful, sunny days.

CHICKEN WINGS
1 teaspoon black peppercorns
2 teaspoons coriander seeds
½ teaspoon cumin seeds
4 garlic cloves
5 sprigs of coriander/cilantro stalks
2 chicken stock cubes, crumbled
3 tablespoons fish sauce
1 kg/2¼ lb. chicken wings
1 litre/4 cups vegetable oil, for frying

DRY MIX
120 g/scant 1 cup self-raising/rising flour
60 g/4 tablespoons rice flour
20 g/scant ¼ cup cornflour/cornstarch
1 teaspoon bicarbonate of/baking soda

GARNISH
200 ml/scant 1 cup vegetable oil
10 garlic cloves, crushed/minced
chopped coriander/cilantro leaves
lime wedges
sweet chilli sauce or other dipping sauce of choice (optional)

SERVES 3–4

Using a pestle and mortar, pound the black peppercorns, coriander seeds and cumin seeds to a fine powder. Add the garlic and coriander stalks, then pound into a smooth paste.

In a large bowl, mix the spice paste with the crumbled chicken stock cubes, fish sauce and 4 tablespoons water. Add the chicken wings and toss well to coat. Cover and marinate in the fridge for at least 1 hour, or preferably overnight.

In a separate bowl, combine the self-raising flour, rice flour, cornflour, and bicarbonate of soda and mix well. Remove the chicken wings from the marinade and shake off any excess. Dredge each wing in the dry mix, making sure each one is evenly coated. Set aside on a wire rack or tray.

To prepare the garnish, heat the vegetable oil in a small pan over a medium heat. Add the garlic and fry until golden brown and crispy. Remove with a slotted spoon and drain on paper towels. Set aside until needed.

Heat the vegetable oil for frying the chicken wings in a large heavy-based pan or deep-fat fryer to 180°C/350°F. Working in batches to avoid overcrowding the pan, deep fry the chicken wings for 7–8 minutes or until golden, crispy and cooked through. Remove with a slotted spoon and drain on paper towels.

Arrange the chicken wings on a serving plate, scatter over the fried garlic and garnish with coriander leaves and lime wedges. Serve with sweet chilli sauce or your favourite dipping sauce.

COOKING TIP Alternatively, preheat the air fryer to 200°C/400°F. Lightly spray the basket with oil. Place the chicken wings in a single layer (cook in batches if needed) and brush a light layer of oil over the wings. Cook for 17–20 minutes, flipping halfway through, until golden brown and crispy.

ลาบไก่
LARB GAI

Thai chicken salad burritos

Larb Gai with a twist! This innovative dish was inspired by a visit to a Mexican restaurant where I ordered a burrito. It sparked the idea to pair the bold flavours of spicy chicken salad with my all-time favourite peanut sauce. The chicken is vibrant and tangy, while the rich and creamy peanut sauce balances the heat, creating the perfect combination.

FILLING
3 tablespoons vegetable oil
3 garlic cloves, crushed/minced
1 red onion, sliced
300 g/10½ oz. minced/ground chicken
3 tablespoons fish sauce
3 tablespoons lime juice
2 tablespoons hot chilli powder
3–4 sprigs of coriander/cilantro, chopped
10 mint leaves, chopped
3 spring onions/scallions, finely chopped

DIPPING SAUCE
4 tablespoons smooth peanut butter
1 tablespoon fish sauce
3 tablespoons hoisin sauce
2 tablespoons lime juice
50 ml/scant ¼ cup hot water
2 garlic cloves, crushed/minced
3 tablespoons sriracha or other hot sauce
3 tablespoons brown sugar
1 tablespoon sesame oil
2 tablespoons honey

TO SERVE
3–4 large white tortillas
1 baby gem lettuce, washed and shredded
2 tomatoes, sliced (or halved cherry tomatoes)
1 cucumber, thinly sliced
handful of coriander/cilantro or Thai basil leaves
1 large red chilli/chile, thinly sliced (optional)

SERVES 3–4

Heat the vegetable oil in a large pan over a medium-high heat. Add the garlic and red onion, then sauté until fragrant. Add the chicken and stir-fry for 5–7 minutes, breaking apart any clumps with a wooden spoon. Season with the fish sauce, lime juice and chilli powder, stirring to mix. Stir in the chopped coriander, mint and spring onions. Adjust the seasoning to taste, balancing the sweet, sour, salt and spicy flavours.

In a microwave-safe bowl, combine all the dipping sauce ingredients. Microwave for 30 seconds to melt the sugar, then mix well until fully combined.

Next, assemble the burritos. Heat a large tortilla in a dry frying pan/skillet over a medium heat for about 30 seconds on each side until soft and pliable. Spread a generous spoonful of the peanut diping sauce across the centre of the tortilla. Add a scoop of the spicy chicken filling on top of the sauce. Top with lettuce, tomatoes, sliced cucumber, coriander and some red chilli, if using.

Fold the sides of the tortilla inward, then roll it tightly from the bottom up, ensuring the filling is secure inside. Slice the burrito in half for easier handling, serve with more of the peanut dipping sauce on the side.

COOKING TIP You can of course also enjoy this Thai-style chicken the more traditional way, served with steamed rice and/or fresh salad vegetables.

Salads & appetizers
สลัดกับของกินเล่น

A tapestry of taste – exploring bold
flavours, vibrant colours and refreshing
combinations of ingredients.

Sesame pork & prawn toasts

Crunchy, golden bites made from a smooth paste of minced/ground pork and prawns/shrimp, which is spread on bread and then deep fried. This is a classic dish that's beloved for its simplicity and flavour. It's the kind of snack you can find at any food market in Thailand, with its crispy exterior and savoury topping. This dish has always been one of my favourites, so I decided to include it on my restaurant menu as an appetizer. It's simple, delicious and the perfect way to start a meal. Whether enjoyed when eating out or at home, it never fails to bring a little taste of Thailand to the table.

200 g/7 oz. minced/ground pork
200 g/7 oz. prawns/shrimp, peeled and deveined
3 garlic cloves
½ a thumb-sized piece of fresh ginger, crushed/minced
½ teaspoon ground white pepper
2 tablespoons sesame oil
2 tablespoons oyster sauce
1 tablespoon caster/superfine sugar
4–5 slices of white bread
1 litre/4 cups vegetable oil, for frying
100 g/3½ oz. sesame seeds, for sprinkling

DIPPING SAUCE
2 large hot red chillies/chiles, finely chopped
4 garlic cloves, crushed/minced
200 g/1 cup caster/superfine sugar
100 g/scant ½ cup cider vinegar
1 teaspoon salt

SERVES 4–8

First, make the dipping sauce. Combine the chillies, garlic, sugar, vinegar and salt in a small saucepan. Bring to a gentle boil, stirring until the sugar dissolves. Simmer for 1–2 minutes, then remove from the heat and set aside to cool.

Next, prepare the toasts. In a food processor, combine the pork, prawns, garlic, ginger, white pepper, sesame oil, oyster sauce and sugar. Blend until smooth and well combined.

Cut the bread slices into triangles, quarters or your preferred shape. Spread a generous layer of the pork and prawn mixture onto each piece, making sure each one is evenly coated. Sprinkle a generous amount of sesame seeds over the top of the coated bread pieces, pressing down lightly so the seeds stick.

Heat the oil in a deep frying pan/skillet or wok over a medium heat. Working in batches to avoid overcrowding the pan, carefully lower the topped bread pieces into the hot oil, paste-side down, and deep fry the toasts for 3–4 minutes, or until golden and crispy. Flip the toasts over and fry on the other side for a further minute. Remove with a slotted spoon and drain on paper towels.

Serve the pork and prawn toasts straight away while hot with the dipping sauce alongside.

ส้มตำสวีด
SWEDE SOM TAM

Thai swede salad

A creative twist on the classic Thai green papaya salad. Green papaya can be difficult to find or expensive to import, so I decided to swap it for shredded swede/rutabaga. Swede has a similar crunchy texture and a neutral flavour, making it a good substitute for green papaya in a spicy salad like this. Here's my take on this classic dish, using a local vegetable to keep it accessible, fresh and just as delicious. This dish is incredibly easy to make, packed with flavour, and requires minimal effort and ingredients. Perfect for any occasion.

200 g/7 oz. swede/rutabaga, finely grated/shredded
1 small carrot, finely grated/shredded
100 g/3½ oz. fine green beans, chopped into 3-cm/1¼-inch pieces
10 cherry tomatoes, halved

DRESSING
2–3 birds eye chillies/chiles, finely chopped
2 garlic cloves, crushed/minced
50 ml/3½ tablespoons lime juice
3 tablespoons fish sauce
4 tablespoons palm sugar (or brown sugar)
2 tablespoons crunchy peanut butter

GARNISH
chopped roasted peanuts (see cooking tip), to garnish (optional)
lime wedges

SERVES 2

First, make the dressing. Combine the birds eye chillies, garlic, lime juice, fish sauce, palm sugar and peanut butter in a mortar and pestle or large bowl (see below), mixing well until the flavours are fully combined.

Put the grated swede and carrot in a mixing bowl, as well as the green beans and cherry tomatoes, along with the dressing. Toss everything together thoroughly. Adjust the seasoning to taste, balancing the sweet, sour, salt and spicy flavours.

Transfer the salad to a serving plate or bowl and garnish with the chopped roasted peanuts (if using) and lime wedges for squeezing over. Serve with sticky rice or grilled meats, if desired.

COOKING TIP To roast peanuts in the oven, preheat the oven to 200°C/180°C fan/200°F/Gas 6. Spread the peanuts out in a single layer on a baking sheet and bake for 10–15 minutes, stirring halfway through for even browning. Remove from the oven and let cool before using.

ลูกชิ้นเนื้อย่าง
LOOK CHIN NUEA YANG

Thai grilled beef meatballs

This was the dish I made during the semi-finals of MasterChef UK, and it's one I'll never forget. I paired the smoky, charred meatballs with a homemade spicy sauce that brought out the best in each other. The feedback was incredible. One of the judges said, 'She kicks like she meant it!' – a comment I proudly took as a compliment to the bold, punchy flavours of my cooking. This dish reflects my love for authentic Thai street food and the vibrant tastes it brings to the table.

MEATBALLS
- 500 g/1 lb 2 oz. minced/ground beef (5% fat)
- 1 teaspoon freshly ground black pepper
- 2 tablespoons caster/superfine sugar
- 1 beef stock cube, crumbled
- 1 teaspoon salt
- 2 tablespoons cornflour/cornstarch
- 2 teaspoons baking powder
- 100 g/3½ oz. ice
- large bowl of ice-cold water

DIPPING SAUCE
- 2 tablespoons dried chilli/hot red pepper flakes
- 4 garlic cloves, crushed/minced
- 3 tablespoons tamarind paste
- 100 g/½ cup brown sugar
- 2 tablespoons fish sauce
- 2 sprigs of coriander/cilantro, chopped
- 50 ml/scant ¼ cup hot water

TO SERVE
- roughly chopped coriander/cilantro leaves
- steamed jasmine or sticky rice
- lettuce leaves, for wrapping
- lime wedges

6–8 bamboo or metal skewers

SERVES 2–3

In a food processor, combine the beef, black pepper, sugar, crumbled stock cube, salt, cornflour and baking powder. Pulse until the mixture is well combined.

Gradually add the ice to the food processor and blend until the mixture becomes smooth, sticky and paler in colour. This step gives the meatballs a firmer texture.

Wet your hands with cold water to prevent sticking. Scoop up a small amount of the beef mixture, about the size of a ping pong ball. Hold it loosely in your hand and gently squeeze it between your thumb and index finger to form a ball that pops out at the top of your fist. Use your other hand to pinch it off and shape it further, if needed. Repeat with the remaining mixture, re-wetting your hands as necessary.

Bring 2 litres/quarts water to the boil in a saucepan. Reduce to a simmer and gently lower the meatballs into the water. Cook for 4–5 minutes or until the meatballs float to the surface. Remove with a slotted spoon and immediately transfer to a bowl of ice-cold water to stop the meatballs cooking and firm up the texture. Drain and set aside until needed.

When ready to cook, heat a grill/broiler or grill pan to a medium heat. Lightly oil the surface to prevent sticking. Thread 3–4 meatballs onto each skewer. Grill the meatballs, turning occasionally, for 6–8 minutes, or until evenly cooked and lightly charred.

Meanwhile, prepare the dipping sauce. Combine all the ingredients in a small bowl. Stir until the sugar dissolves and everything is well mixed.

Serve the grilled meatballs straight away while hot garnished with coriander and lime wedges for squeezing over. Accompany the meatballs with rice and/or lettuce leaves, as preferred, and the dipping sauce.

ปอเปี๊ยะทอดใส่มันฝรั่งบด
POR PIA TOD

Bubble & squeak spring rolls
with sweet chilli sauce

Crispy spring rolls filled with a classic bubble and squeak mix of cabbage and potatoes, served with sweet chilli sauce. I originally created this dish for the MasterChef UK competition, but I didn't get the chance to showcase it. I love combining elements from East and West, and this dish is a perfect example of that fusion.

These spring rolls are a crowd-pleaser – crispy on the outside with a soft, flavourful filling inside. Whether served as an appetizer or a fun party snack, they never fail to impress. It's a dish that brings together familiar flavours in an exciting way, offering a satisfying crunch with every bite, making it perfect for enjoying with friends and family.

SPRING ROLLS
- 1 tablespoon butter
- 150 g/5½ oz. unsmoked bacon rashers, chopped
- 1 onion, sliced
- 3 garlic cloves, crushed/minced
- 200 g/7 oz. Savoy cabbage, shredded
- 400 g/14 oz. cooked mashed potatoes
- ½ teaspoon freshly ground black pepper
- 200 g/7 oz. spring roll pastry wrappers (not the Vietnamese spring roll rice wrappers)
- 500 ml/2 cups vegetable oil, for frying

SWEET CHILLI SAUCE
- 2 large hot red chillies/chiles, finely chopped
- 4 garlic cloves, crushed/minced
- 200 g/1 cup caster/superfine sugar
- 100 g/scant ½ cup cider vinegar
- 1 teaspoon salt

MAKE 6–8 SPRING ROLLS

To make the sweet chilli sauce, combine all the ingredients in a saucepan. Bring to the boil over a medium heat, stirring occasionally, until the sugar dissolves. Lower the heat and simmer for 5–7 minutes, or until the sauce thickens slightly. Remove from heat and set aside to cool.

Next, prepare the spring roll filling. In a large pan, melt the butter over a medium heat. Add the chopped bacon and cook for 3–4 minutes, or until it becomes crispy and releases its fat. Add the onion and garlic and stir-fry for 2–3 minutes until softened and fragrant.

Stir in the shredded cabbage and cook for 3–4 minutes until wilted. Add the mashed potatoes and black pepper, stirring everything together until well combined. Cook for a further 2 minutes, then remove from the heat and let it cool slightly.

To assemble the spring rolls, place a spring roll pastry wrapper on a clean work surface. Place about 2 tablespoons of the filling near one corner of the wrapper. Fold the corner of the wrapper over the filling, then fold in the sides and roll everything up tightly. Seal the edge with a little water. Repeat with the remaining wrappers and filling.

Heat the oil in a heavy-based pan over a medium-high heat. Working in batches to avoid overcrowding the pan, carefully lower the spring rolls into the hot oil and deep fry for 3–4 minutes or until golden and crispy. Remove with a slotted spoon and drain on paper towels.

Serve the spring rolls, cut in half, with the sweet chilli sauce on the side.

SAI UA SCOTCH EGGS

Sai ua scotch eggs

An innovative fusion of a traditional northern Thai dish, *Sai ua*, and the classic English scotch egg. This light snack combines the bold flavours of *Sai ua* sausage with the gooey texture of a runny yolk, making it a tasty treat. I love this dish because it blends Western cuisine with the food I ate when I was growing up in Chiang Mai – and it tastes great too!

4 medium/US large free-range eggs
splash of vinegar
2 garlic cloves
1 small shallot
coin-sized piece of galangal (or thumb-sized piece of fresh ginger)
1 lemongrass stalk, finely chopped
400 g/14 oz. minced/ground pork
½ teaspoon ground turmeric
2 tablespoons fish sauce
20 g/¾ oz. coriander/cilantro, stalks and leaves finely chopped
2 makrut lime leaves, finely chopped (you can use dried ones, but they need to be soaked first)
4 teaspoons dried chilli/hot red pepper flakes
4 teaspoons paprika
1 litre/4 cups vegetable oil, for frying
salad and sweet chilli sauce, to serve (optional)

TO COAT
200 g/1½ cups plain/all-purpose flour
2 large/US extra-large eggs, beaten
200 g/4 cups panko breadcrumbs

MAKES 4 SCOTCH EGGS

To soft boil the eggs, bring a saucepan of water to the boil. Add the eggs with a splash of vinegar (to help with peeling later) and simmer for 6 minutes. Immediately transfer the eggs to a bowl of cold water to stop the cooking process. Carefully peel the eggs and set aside in the fridge.

Place the garlic, shallot, galangal and lemongrass in a mortar and use the pestle to grind to a fine paste. (I use a mortar and pestle to make the paste, but you can use a food processor, if you prefer.)

In a mixing bowl, combine the spice paste with the pork, turmeric, fish sauce, coriander, lime leaves, chilli flakes and paprika. Mix well.

On a flat work surface, lay down some cling film/plastic wrap, then add around 100 g/3½ oz. of the pork mixture. Press it down either by hand or using a rolling pin to about 5 mm/¼ inch thick. Place a soft-boiled egg in the centre of the pork and gently wrap the meat mixture around the egg so that it is completely covered.

Prepare the coating by placing the flour, beaten eggs and panko breadcrumbs in three separate containers or shallow dishes.

Meanwhile, heat the vegetable oil in a deep heavy-based saucepan or frying pan/skillet. Ensure there is enough oil to cover the eggs.

Coat the scotch eggs in flour first, then in the beaten eggs and finally in panko breadcrumbs. Working in batches to avoid overcrowding the pan, carefully lower the scotch eggs into the hot oil and deep fry for 5–6 minutes, turning occasionally to ensure even browning, or until golden and crispy.

Remove with a slotted spoon and drain on paper towels to absorb any excess oil. Cut in half and serve with a fresh side salad and sweet chilli sauce for drizzling.

บัตเตอร์นัทสควอชทอด
BUTTERNUT SQUASH TOD

Spiced butternut squash fritters with lime yogurt dip

This is my go-to summer snack, and it's always a hit! Traditionally, we use pumpkin for this recipe back in Thailand, but after moving here, I found that butternut squash is a perfect substitute – it's easy to find and works just as well. These fritters are crispy on the outside, soft on the inside and packed with fragrant Thai spices that make them so moreish. Whether you're enjoying them as a quick snack or serving them up for friends and family, they always disappear fast!

Paired with a refreshing lime yogurt dip, the combination of crunchy, spiced fritters with the cool, tangy dip makes for a perfect balance of flavours – great for warm, sunny days or when you're craving something light yet satisfying.

1 butternut squash
200 g/1½ cups plain/all-purpose flour
½ teaspoon salt
1 teaspoon ground cinnamon
1 teaspoon dried chilli/hot red pepper flakes
½ teaspoon ground coriander
½ teaspoon ground cumin
2 teaspoons baking powder
2 tablespoons caster/superfine sugar
2 large/US extra-large eggs
500 ml/2 cups vegetable oil, for frying

LIME YOGURT DIP
200 g/1 scant cup full-fat Greek yogurt
zest and juice of 1 lime
2 garlic cloves, crushed/minced
½ teaspoon salt

MAKES 12–14 FRITTERS

Peel and grate the butternut squash into a large mixing bowl.

In a separate bowl, whisk together the flour, salt, cinnamon, chilli flakes, coriander, cumin, baking powder and sugar until well combined. Add the grated butternut squash to the dry ingredients and mix well.

In another bowl, beat the eggs, then pour them into the butternut squash mixture. Stir until everything is evenly combined and forms a thick batter.

Heat the vegetable oil in a deep, heavy-based pan over a medium heat. Working in batches to avoid overcrowding the pan, carefully drop small portions of the batter into the hot oil and deep fry for about 3–4 minutes, or until the fritters are golden brown and crispy. Remove with a slotted spoon and drain on paper towels.

To make the dip, in a small bowl, mix the Greek yogurt, lime zest, lime juice, garlic and salt. Stir well until smooth and creamy.

Serve the crispy fritters straight away while hot with the lime yogurt dip.

ขนมจีบใส้หมู
KANOM JEEB SAI MOO

Pork dumplings

This dish is one of the most popular starters at my restaurant, and for good reason! I started making these pork dumplings because I couldn't find a good version after moving to England, and I wanted to recreate the flavours that I loved from my childhood. I still remember how special it felt to have a few pieces when I was a kid – each bite was delicious, but they were considered quite expensive back then. Now, I get to share these dumplings with my customers, made with homemade wonton wrappers and filled with a flavourful pork mixture that's juicy and perfectly seasoned.

WONTON WRAPPERS
300 g/generous 2 cups strong white flour
2 tablespoons cornflour/cornstarch, plus extra for dusting
½ teaspoon salt
1 large/US extra-large egg, lightly beaten

PORK FILLING
500 g/1 lb 2 oz. minced/ground pork (20% fat)
3 coriander/cilantro stalks, crushed/minced
4 garlic cloves, crushed/minced
½ teaspoon ground white pepper
2 teaspoons caster/superfine sugar
1 tablespoon sesame oil
2 tablespoons light soy sauce
2–3 spring onions/scallions, chopped

DIPPING SAUCE
3 tablespoons light soy sauce
1 tablespoon dark soy sauce
2 tablespoons brown sugar
2 tablespoons cider vinegar
2 tablespoons hot water
2 birds eye chillies/chiles, finely chopped
2 garlic cloves, crushed/minced
½ a thumb-size piece of fresh ginger, crushed/minced

8-cm/3¼-inch cookie cutter (or a glass rim)
steamer lined with parchment paper

MAKE 15–20 DUMPLINGS

First, make the wonton wrappers. In a mixing bowl, combine the strong white flour, cornflour and salt. Gradually add the lightly beaten egg and 75 ml/⅓ cup cold water while mixing. Knead the dough for about 8–10 minutes, or until smooth and elastic. Cover with a damp cloth and let it rest for 30 minutes.

For the dipping sauce, in a small bowl, mix together both soy sauces, the brown sugar, cider vinegar and hot water until the sugar dissolves. Stir in the chillies, garlic and ginger. Set aside.

Lightly dust a clean work surface with cornflour. Roll out the dough as thinly as possible, then use the cookie cutter or glass rim to punch out discs. Dust each one with a little cornflour to prevent sticking. Set aside while you prepare the filling.

For the filling, in a large bowl, combine the pork, coriander, garlic, white pepper, sugar, sesame oil, light soy sauce and spring onions. Mix well until fully combined and slightly sticky.

Place a heaped tablespoon of the filling in the centre of a wonton wrapper, then gently gather and pleat the edges of the wrapper around the filling. Use your fingers to press and shape it into a small, open-top dumpling. The top of the filling should remain exposed, while the sides are gently wrapped. Repeat until all the wrappers and filling are used.

Working in batches if needed, arrange the dumplings in the steamer so they are not touching. Steam for 8–10 minutes, or until the filling is cooked through. Serve the dumplings straight away while hot with the dipping sauce on the side.

Crispy prawn & lemongrass wontons

This dish is one of my all-time favourite snacks, and it's been a popular appetizer at my restaurant as well. The combination of fresh prawns/shrimp, fragrant lemongrass and crispy wonton wrappers makes it so light, crunchy and absolutely delicious.

What I love most about this recipe is how easy it is to make at home. It's perfect for a fun family activity on the weekend, where everyone can help with wrapping and frying the wontons. Whether served as a snack, appetizer or party food, they're guaranteed to be a hit with both kids and adults.

1 quantity of Wonton Wrappers (see page 56)
500 g/1 lb 2 oz. prawns/shrimp, peeled and deveined
3 coriander/cilantro sprigs, very finely chopped
4 garlic cloves, crushed/minced
1 lemongrass stalk, crushed/minced
½ teaspoon ground white pepper
2 teaspoons caster/superfine sugar
1 tablespoon sesame oil
2 tablespoons light soy sauce
2–3 spring onions/scallions, chopped
500 ml/2 cups vegetable oil, for frying

8-cm/3¼-inch cookie cutter (or a glass rim)

MAKE 15–20 WONTONS

First, make the wonton wrappers following the instructions on page 56. Lightly dust a clean work surface with cornflour. Roll out the dough as thinly as possible, then use the cookie cutter or glass rim to punch out discs. Dust each wrapper with a little more cornflour to prevent sticking. Set aside while you prepare the filling.

For the filling, finely chop the prawns, then place in a mixing bowl. Add the coriander, garlic, lemongrass, white pepper, sugar, sesame oil, light soy sauce and spring onions. Mix well until fully combined.

Place a teaspoon of the prawn filling in the centre of a wonton wrapper. Moisten the edges of the wrapper with water, then fold over the filling to make a semi-circle, pressing to seal the edges. Bring the ends round to meet and create a parcel, pressing to seal in place (see the image on the previous page). Repeat until all the wrappers and filling are used.

Heat the vegetable oil in a deep heavy-based pan or wok over a medium heat. Working in batches to avoid overcrowding the pan, deep fry the wontons for 3–4 minutes, or until golden brown and crispy. Remove with a slotted spoon and drain on paper towels.

Serve the crispy wontons straight away while hot with your favourite dipping sauce, such as sweet chilli sauce (see page 51) or a chilli and lime dipping sauce (see page 64).

SALAD TAENG MO

Watermelon salad
with Thai basil & mint

This refreshing and vibrant salad is perfect for a hot day or as a light, flavourful side dish. The sweetness of juicy watermelon, paired with fragrant Thai basil and fresh mint, creates a delicious balance of flavours that's both cooling and satisfying. The combination of sweet, salty and tangy makes this salad stand out, and it's super quick and easy to put together. Whether you're serving it at a summer barbecue, a casual lunch or as a refreshing snack, it's guaranteed to be a crowd-pleaser.

1 small watermelon, peeled and cut into bite-sized pieces
1 small onion, thinly sliced
2 tablespoons roasted peanuts (see page 47), crushed
1–2 sprigs of Thai basil leaves, coarsely chopped
6–7 mint leaves, torn

DRESSING
3 tablespoons lime juice
3 tablespoon fish sauce
1 tablespoon brown sugar
1 teaspoon dried chilli/hot red pepper flakes

SERVES 2–3

First, prepare the dressing. In a small bowl, whisk together the lime juice, fish sauce, brown sugar and dried chilli flakes until the sugar dissolves and the flavours are well combined.

In a large bowl, place the watermelon and onion. Sprinkle over the crushed roasted peanuts, followed by the chopped basil and torn mint.

Pour the dressing over the watermelon salad and gently toss everything together to ensure the flavours are evenly distributed. Serve immediately.

COOKING TIP To choose the best tasting watermelon, give the watermelon a firm tap – a deep, hollow sound means it's juicy and ripe.

ปลาหมึกย่าง
PLA MEUK YANG

Grilled squid
with chilli & lime dipping sauce

This dish takes me right back to the winter festivals in Thailand, where I loved stopping by street-food vendors selling freshly grilled squid with a spicy dipping sauce. The smoky aroma of the charred squid and the punchy, tangy sauce always made it the perfect snack to enjoy while wandering through the bustling festival crowds.

Since moving away, I recreate this dish to relive those cherished memories and bring a taste of those festive Thai winters back into my life. The squid is tender and lightly charred, and when dipped into the spicy, zesty sauce, it's an explosion of flavours that always reminds me of home.

½ teaspoon coriander seeds, ground to a fine powder
2 tablespoons olive oil
1 teaspoon paprika
½ teaspoon salt
½ teaspoon freshly ground black pepper
2–3 squid, gutted and cleaned
lime wedges, to serve

DIPPING SAUCE
1 large hot red chilli/chile, very finely chopped
3 garlic cloves, minced
2–3 coriander/cilantro sprigs, finely chopped
1 small shallot, finely chopped
3 tablespoons lime juice
3 tablespoons fish sauce
2 tablespoons hot water
1 tablespoon brown sugar

SERVES 2–3

In a mixing bowl, combine the ground coriander seeds, olive oil, paprika, salt and black pepper. Add the cleaned squid to the bowl and toss well to coat evenly with the marinade. Leave for at least 20 minutes to absorb the flavours.

Preheat a grill/broiler or grill pan over a medium-high heat. Once hot, place the squid on the grill and cook for 2–3 minutes on each side, or until lightly charred and just cooked through. Avoid overcooking to keep the squid tender.

In a small bowl, combine the red chilli, garlic, coriander and shallot. Add the lime juice, fish sauce, hot water and brown sugar, stirring until the sugar is fully dissolved. Adjust the seasoning to taste, balancing the sweet, sour, salty and spicy flavours.

Serve the grilled squid straight away while hot, alongside the spicy dipping sauce.

COOKING TIP Always use fresh squid, rather than frozen. I prefer larger-size squid for grilling as they stay tender and juicy.

Crying tiger beef salad

Crying tiger beef salad is a dish as intriguing as its name. This dish is beloved for celebrations and special occasions, partly because steak is considered a luxury in Thailand, making it a rare and meaningful treat. The tender grilled beef, paired with bold, spicy and tangy flavours, turns every bite into something extraordinary. Its rarity makes it even more special, and it's a dish everyone loves to share when marking life's big moments.

200–300 g/7–10 oz. sirloin steak
pinch of salt and black pepper
3 tablespoons vegetable oil
200 g/7 oz. baby gem lettuce, to serve

DRESSING
2 tablespoons dried chilli/hot red pepper flakes
3 tablespoons lime juice
3 tablespoons fish sauce
1 teaspoon brown sugar
1 red onion, sliced
1 large hot red chilli/chile, thinly sliced
100 g/3½ oz. cherry tomatoes, halved
a handful of coriander/cilantro, stalks and leaves chopped, plus extra to garnish
3 spring onions/scallions, thinly sliced

SERVES 1–2

Season the steak with a pinch of salt and black pepper on both sides. Heat the vegetable oil in a frying pan/skillet over a medium-high heat. Once hot, sear the steak for 2–3 minutes on each side for medium-rare, or adjust the cooking time to your preference. Remove the steak from the pan and let it rest for 5 minutes before slicing thinly into strips.

Meanwhile, prepare the dressing. In a mixing bowl, combine the dried chilli flakes, lime juice, fish sauce and brown sugar. Stir until the sugar is dissolved. Add the red onion, red chilli, cherry tomatoes, chopped coriander and spring onions, then toss gently to combine.

Arrange the baby gem lettuce leaves on a serving platter. Lay the sliced steak on the lettuce, then spoon the dressing evenly over the top and garnish with some extra coriander if liked. Serve immediately.

COOKING TIP Use a sirloin steak with an even thickness to achieve perfectly medium-rare meat once cooked.

Soups & broths
น้ำซุปและแกง

Fragrant delights – discover fresh
and aromatic recipes from around
the country.

TOM YUM GOONG

Thai hot & sour soup with prawns

Tom yum soup is a national favourite that almost everyone in Thailand knows how to make, and every family seems to have their own recipe. I love cooking this dish as it's connected to a special memory for me when the movie *Tom yum goong* came out. It's my favourite action movie, showcasing Thai boxing and the culture of Northern Thailand, where I'm from. I still remember watching it for the first time on TV with my mum and brother. We had a big pot of *tom yum* soup on the table, and the flavours made the experience even more unforgettable.

1 litre/4 cups chicken stock (homemade or from stock cubes)
4 tablespoons chilli paste (see below)
4 tablespoons fish sauce
4 tablespoons lime juice
1 lemongrass stalk, cut into long thin slices
2 birds eye chillies/chiles, bruised
½ a thumb-sized piece of galangal, sliced (or fresh ginger)
4 makrut lime leaves
100 g/3½ oz. oyster mushrooms, torn into bite-sized pieces
100 g/3½ oz. cherry tomatoes, halved
1 red onion, thinly sliced
200 g/7 oz. king prawns/jumbo shrimp, peeled and deveined
100 ml/scant ½ cup evaporated milk
handful of coriander/cilantro, stalks and leaves chopped
2–3 spring onions/scallions, chopped

CHILLI PASTE
10 large dried red chillies/chiles
3 small shallots, quartered
6 garlic cloves, halved
1 lemongrass stalk, chopped
½ a thumb-size piece of galangal, sliced (or fresh ginger)
200 ml/scant 1 cup vegetable oil
3 tablespoons tamarind paste
4 tablespoons brown sugar
2 teaspoons salt

SERVES 3–4

First, make the chilli paste. Soak the dried chillies in warm water for 10 minutes, then drain, but keep the water. Using a food processor or mortar and pestle, grind the soaked chilies, shallots, garlic, lemongrass and galangal into a smooth paste. If blending is difficult, add a few tablespoons of the reserved soaking water at a time to help create a smooth paste.

Heat the vegetable oil in a frying pan/skillet over a medium heat. Add the paste and sauté for 5–7 minutes until fragrant. Stir in the tamarind paste, brown sugar and salt. Cook for about 2 minutes, then remove from the heat. Set aside until needed.

In a large saucepan, bring the chicken stock to a gentle boil over a medium heat. Add 4 tablespoons of the prepared chilli paste, the fish sauce and lime juice. Stir well. Add the lemongrass, bruised chillies, galangal and lime leaves, then simmer for about 5 minutes to infuse the broth with their flavours.

Add the oyster mushrooms, cherry tomatoes and red onion to the pan. Simmer for a further 5 minutes, or until the vegetables are tender. Add the prawns and cook for 2–3 minutes, or until cooked through. Stir in the evaporated milk for a creamy finish. Adjust the seasoning to taste with more lime juice, fish sauce or chilli paste, if needed.

Ladle the soup into deep bowls and garnish with chopped coriander and spring onions.

ต้มข่าไก่
TOM KHA GAI

Spicy coconut soup with chicken

Tom kha gai was always one of my favourite childhood dishes. I used to eat it at school in Thailand, where we had to buy our own lunch from the canteen. There were several food stalls, and you could choose whatever you liked. I was always grateful to have just enough money for lunch each day, although I sometimes wished I could afford a fruit juice or a sweet treat afterwards.

Anyway, back to the recipe! This dish is pure comfort. It's not overly spicy but has a warm, creamy richness from the coconut milk, balanced by bold flavours from the herbs and spices. It's the perfect meal for a chilly day. You can enjoy it with boiled rice or on its own. Either way, it's a bowl of warmth and coziness!

1 litre/4 cups chicken stock (homemade or from stock cubes)
2 lemongrass stalks, cut into long thin slices
thumb-sized piece of galangal, thinly sliced
1 red onion, thinly sliced
3 large red chillies/chiles, cut into long thin slices
4 makrut lime leaves, torn into small pieces
500 g/1 lb 2 oz. skinless and boneless chicken thighs, cut into 2.5-cm/1-inch pieces
400 ml/14 fl oz. coconut milk
1 teaspoon salt
50 ml/3½ tablespoons fish sauce
75 ml/⅓ cup lime juice
3 tablespoons palm sugar (or brown sugar)
100 g/3½ oz. oyster mushrooms, torn into bite-sized pieces
¼ head sweetheart cabbage or white cabbage, roughly sliced
5 sprigs of coriander/cilantro, stalks and leaves finely chopped
3 spring onions/scallions, finely chopped

SERVES 2–3

In a large saucepan, bring the chicken stock to a gentle simmer over a medium-low heat. Add the lemongrass, galangal, red onion, red chillies and lime leaves and simmer for 10 minutes to release the aromas and flavours of the herbs.

Add the chicken pieces, stirring occasionally to prevent sticking and cook for a further 5 minutes, or until the chicken is fully cooked.

Stir in the coconut milk, then season the soup with the salt, fish sauce, lime juice and palm sugar and reduce the heat to low. Add the oyster mushrooms and cabbage, letting the soup simmer for 2–3 minutes.

Taste the soup and adjust the seasoning, balancing the sweet, sour, salty and spicy flavours. Turn off the heat and stir in the coriander and spring onions. Once you're satisfied with the flavours, ladle the soup into deep bowls and serve immediately while hot.

COOKING TIP Avoid covering the soup with a lid once the coriander and spring onion have been added to prevent them from overcooking and turning yellow.

TOM SAAP MOO

Tangy & spicy pork broth

There was a tiny hidden hot spring waterfall deep in the mountains near a neighbouring village, and my mum, my brother and I would visit it from time to time. The three of us would squeeze onto our motorcycle and ride off on an adventure. I remember stopping at a small street-food stall on one of those trips and ordering *tom saap moo*. It was so delicious – whether it was the flavours or the excitement of the trip, I'm not sure. Every time I eat it now, that memory comes rushing back, making the dish even more special.

When I was young, I always thought of *tom saap moo* as the pork version of *tom yum*, but with flavours more in the eastern Thai style.

1 litre/4 cups chicken stock (homemade or from stock cubes)
1 lemongrass stalk, cut into long thin slices
½ a thumb-sized piece of galangal, sliced
4 makrut lime leaves, torn
500 g/1 lb 2 oz. pork belly, thinly sliced
50 g/1¾ oz. oyster mushrooms, torn into bite-sized pieces
100 g/3½ oz. cherry tomatoes, halved
1 red onion, thinly sliced
3 tablespoons dried chilli/hot red pepper flakes
3 tablespoons fish sauce
4 tablespoons lime juice
½ teaspoon salt
3–4 sprigs of coriander/cilantro, stalks and leaves chopped
2–3 spring onions/scallions, chopped
steamed rice, to serve

SERVES 2–3

In a large saucepan, bring the chicken stock to the boil over a medium heat. Add the lemongrass, galangal and lime leaves and simmer for 5 minutes to release the aromas and flavours of the herbs.

Add the sliced pork belly and cook for 10–15 minutes, or until the pork is tender.

Stir in the oyster mushrooms, cherry tomatoes and red onion and simmer for a further 5 minutes, or until the vegetables are softened.

Season the soup with dried chilli flakes, fish sauce, lime juice and salt. Taste the soup and adjust the seasoning, balancing the sweet, sour, salty and spicy flavours.

Turn off the heat and stir in the coriander and spring onions. Serve immediately while hot and enjoy with a bowl of steamed rice!

COOKING TIP Using homemade chicken stock always gives the best flavour to soups and broths, but you can use stock cubes dissolved in boiling water for convenience if preferred.

ก๋วยเตี๋ยวเนื้อต้มยำ
GUEY TEAW NUA TOM YUM

Spicy beef broth with rice noodles

Tom yum is one of the most iconic dishes of Thailand, celebrated for its hot, spicy, bold and tangy flavours. In this version, I've chosen to use beef, as its rich flavour pairs beautifully with the bold and aromatic broth. Growing up, this was my go-to dish at the local street-food stalls when picking up dinner. After moving to the UK, I started recreating it at home, refining the recipe through trial and error. Now, I'm excited to share my version with you.

3 tablespoons vegetable oil
1 tablespoon dried chilli/hot red pepper flakes
1 litre/4 cups beef stock (homemade or from stock cubes)
2 lemongrass stalks, cut into long thin slices
thumb-sized piece of galangal, thinly sliced
4 makrut lime leaves, torn into small pieces
3 garlic cloves, crushed
2 small shallots, crushed
1 teaspoon salt
75 ml/5 tablespoons lime juice
3 tablespoons fish sauce
1 teaspoon palm sugar (or brown sugar)
2 sprigs of coriander/cilantro, stalks and leaves finely chopped
2 spring onions/scallions, finely chopped
200 g/7 oz. beef rump/top sirloin steak, thinly sliced
1 pak choi/bok choy, quartered or chopped into smaller pieces (optional)
200 g/7 oz. rice noodles
1 litre/4 cups boiling water

SERVES 2–3

Heat the oil in a large saucepan over a medium-high heat. Add the dried chilli flakes, reduce the heat to low and stir continuously for 2–3 minutes to release the aroma and flavour of the chilli flakes.

Add the beef stock, lemongrass, galangal, lime leaves, garlic and shallots to the pan. Simmer over a medium heat for 10 minutes, stirring occasionally to prevent anything from sticking to the bottom of the pan.

Season the broth with the salt, lime juice, fish sauce and palm sugar. Stir in the coriander and spring onions. Taste the broth and adjust the seasoning, balancing the sweet, sour, salty and spicy flavours.

Add the thinly sliced steak and pak choi and cook for 1 minute over a medium heat, ensuring the steak remains tender and not overcooked. Turn off the heat.

In a medium bowl, place the rice noodles and cover them with the boiling water. Stir immediately and let them soak for 3–4 minutes. Test the noodles by cutting a strand with a spoon; if there are no white spots in the centre, they are ready. If soaking alone doesn't soften the noodles, cook them on the hob for 2–3 minutes instead (adjusting the cooking time based on the type of noodles used).

Divide the drained noodles between two deep bowls, then ladle the hot beef broth over them.

Rice soup

Khao tom gai is my ultimate comfort food, especially when I'm feeling under the weather. There's something so soothing about a warm pot of this chicken and rice soup – it's cozy, delicious and perfect for a cold, rainy day. Even though I live in England now, eating khao tom gai always makes me feel like I'm back home in Thailand. It's a dish that brings me comfort no matter where I am.

240 g/8 oz. jasmine rice
3 tablespoons vegetable oil
6 garlic cloves, crushed/minced
100 g/3½ oz. fennel bulb, thinly sliced
200 g/7 oz. chicken breast, thinly sliced
2 litres/quarts chicken stock (homemade or from stock cubes)
4 tablespoons light soy sauce
2 teaspoons salt
1 teaspoon ground white pepper
2 eggs, lightly beaten
thumb-size piece of fresh ginger, sliced into thin matchsticks

GARNISH
chopped coriander/cilantro leaves
3–4 spring onions/scallions, chopped

SERVES 2–3

Rinse the jasmine rice under cold water until the water runs clear. Set aside until needed.

Heat the vegetable oil in a large saucepan over a medium heat. Add the garlic and fennel and sauté for 2–3 minutes, or until fragrant and slightly softened.

Add the chicken to the pan and stir-fry for 3–4 minutes until just cooked, then remove from the pan and set aside.

Pour in the chicken stock and bring it to the boil. Stir in the jasmine rice, lower the heat to a gentle simmer and cook for 45–50 minutes until the rice is tender, stirring occasionally to prevent the rice sticking to the bottom of the pan.

Add the soy sauce, salt and white pepper, then stir well to incorporate. Taste and adjust the seasoning as needed. Add the cooked chicken back into the pan for the final 5 minutes of the cooking time to warm it through without overcooking. Stir well to combine.

Slowly drizzle the beaten eggs into the soup, while gently stirring, to create delicate egg ribbons. Add the ginger and simmer for a further 2–3 minutes.

Ladle the soup into deep bowls and garnish with chopped coriander and spring onions. Serve immediately while hot.

สุกี้น้ำใส่เต้าหู้
SUKI NAM SAI TAO HOO

Thai-style suki yaki with tofu

Growing up, going to the shopping mall to eat at MK Suki was always a special treat or a way to celebrate. This restaurant has been around for over 50 years, and it's a beloved franchise where every branch serves the same familiar flavours. Their secret weapon? The signature suki yaki sauce – it's what makes them stand out. I've created my own version of the famous sauce – it's not exactly the same as MK Suki, but it's close enough to bring back those cherished childhood memories.

1 litre/4 cups chicken stock (homemade or from stock cubes)
3 garlic cloves, bruised
4 tablespoons light soy sauce
2 tablespoons oyster sauce
½ teaspoon ground white pepper
2 celery sticks/ribs, sliced
3–4 Chinese cabbage leaves, chopped
200 g/7 oz. pak choi/bok choy, chopped
1 small carrot, sliced
2–3 chestnut mushrooms, thinly sliced
2 large/US extra-large eggs, lightly beaten
100 g/3½ oz. glass noodles, soaked in water for 10–15 minutes, then drained
200 g/7 oz. soft tofu, cut into cubes
3–4 spring onions/scallions, chopped
3–4 sprigs of coriander/cilantro, stalks and leaves chopped

SUKI YAKI SAUCE
100 g/scant ½ cup sriracha or other hot sauce
200 g/scant 1 cup tomato ketchup
4 tablespoons brown sugar
4 garlic cloves, crushed/minced
4 birds eye chillies/chiles, finely chopped
3 sprigs of coriander/cilantro, stalks and leaves chopped separately
3 tablespoons sesame oil
2 tablespoons oyster sauce
1 tablespoon light soy sauce
3 tablespoons lime juice
1 tablespoon white sesame seeds, toasted

SERVES 2–3

In a large saucepan, bring the chicken stock (or water with stock cubes) to the boil over a medium heat. Add the garlic and let it simmer for 5 minutes to infuse the broth with flavour.

Stir in the soy sauce, oyster sauce and white pepper. Add the celery, Chinese cabbage, pak choi, carrot and mushrooms and cook for 5 minutes, or until the vegetables start to soften.

Slowly drizzle the beaten eggs into the soup, while gently stirring, to create delicate egg ribbons.

Add the soaked glass noodles and soft tofu, then simmer for a further 2–3 minutes until everything is heated through. Turn off the heat and stir in the spring onions and coriander.

To make the sauce, in a mixing bowl, combine the sriracha sauce, tomato ketchup, brown sugar, garlic, chillies and chopped coriander stalks. Add the sesame oil, oyster sauce, soy sauce and lime juice and stir well until fully combined. Finish by mixing in the toasted sesame seeds and finely chopped coriander leaves for an extra burst of flavour.

Serve the soup immediately while hot with a little suki yaki sauce drizzled over the top and extra on the side.

COOKING TIP To make this a vegetarian dish just replace oyster sauce to vegan oyster sauce and use vegetable stock instead of chicken stock.

Mixed seafood clear soup

I have to say, *gaeng jued talay* must be every kid's favourite school meal back home. We absolutely loved our school lunches! I know it might sound odd because everyone seems to complain about their school meals, but for us, it was the opposite. We were so lucky to have such tasty food at school – sometimes even better than what we had at home.

Looking back, maybe it was because we didn't have much, and life back then wasn't easy. But this dish was always a comforting treat – packed with protein, lots of vegetables and, best of all, no spice, which made it perfect for kids. That's probably why we all loved it so much!

1 litre/4 cups chicken stock (homemade or from stock cubes)
3 garlic cloves, bruised
1 small fennel bulb, chopped into bite-sized pieces
4 tablespoons light soy sauce
2 tablespoons oyster sauce
½ teaspoon ground white pepper
200 g/7 oz. mixed seafood (such as prawns/shrimp, squid, mussels)
3–4 Chinese cabbage leaves, chopped into bite-sized pieces
100 g/3½ oz. soft tofu, cut into bite-sized pieces
100 g/3½ oz. glass noodles, soaked in water for 10–15 minutes, then drained
3–4 spring onions/scallions, chopped
3–4 sprigs of coriander/cilantro, stalks and leaves chopped
steamed jasmine rice, to serve (optional)

SERVES 2–3

In a large saucepan, bring the chicken stock (or water with stock cubes) to the boil over a medium heat.

Add the garlic and fennel and let it simmer for 5 minutes to release their flavours. Stir in the soy sauce, oyster sauce and white pepper.

Add the mixed seafood and cook for 3–4 minutes, or until it turns opaque and cooked through. Add the Chinese cabbage and soft tofu, letting them simmer for a further 3 minutes.

Gently add the soaked glass noodles and cook for a further 2 minutes, just until they soften and absorb the flavours. Turn off the heat and stir in the spring onions and coriander.

Serve immediately while hot with jasmine rice or enjoy on its own for a light and comforting meal.

Thai chicken noodle broth

I loved this dish when I was a kid because it had no chilli and was always so soothing to eat. In our family, we usually had this dish at lunchtime. On days when my grandad or mum didn't feel like cooking, they would hand me some money to buy lunch from the food stall nearby. I'd hop on my bicycle, ride to the stall and come back with this warm, delicious meal. I really miss those days – playing outside all morning until I was starving, then riding my bike to grab lunch and enjoying every bite. It's amazing how small moments like these can turn into such special memories that stay with you forever.

1 litre/4 cups chicken stock (homemade or from stock cubes)
500 g/1 lb 2 oz. chicken legs or drumsticks
3 garlic cloves, bruised
3–4 sprigs of coriander/cilantro stalks, torn
4 tablespoons light soy sauce
2 tablespoons oyster sauce
½ teaspoon ground white pepper
200 g/7 oz. rice noodles
handful of beansprouts
100 g/3½ oz. pak choi/bok choy, cut into bite-sized pieces
2–3 spring onions/scallions, chopped
2–3 sprigs of coriander/cilantro, stalks and leaves chopped

ADDITIONAL FLAVOURINGS
caster/superfine sugar
fish sauce
cider vinegar
dried chilli/hot red pepper flakes

SERVES 2–3

In a large saucepan, bring the chicken stock (or water with stock cubes) to the boil over a medium heat. Add the chicken drumsticks, bruised garlic and torn coriander stalks. Let it simmer for 30–40 minutes, or until the chicken is tender and the broth is full of flavour.

Stir in the light soy sauce, oyster sauce and white pepper and let it simmer for a further 5 minutes.

While the broth is cooking, soak the rice noodles in hot water for 5–10 minutes until softened, then drain and set aside.

When ready to serve, divide the drained rice noodles, beansprouts and pak choi between two deep bowls. Pour the hot chicken broth over the noodles, making sure to include some chicken pieces. Top with chopped spring onion and coriander.

Serve the soup with additional flavourings alongside, such as sugar, fish sauce, cider vinegar and dried chilli flakes, allowing everyone to adjust the taste to their personal preference.

แกงส้มปลาซาวมอล
GAENG SOM SALMON

Sour curry soup

Gaeng som salmon is my mum's favourite dish. She loves incredibly spicy food, and this thin curry, more like a spicy broth, ticks all the boxes for her. Over time, I've tweaked the recipe to make it less spicy than the version I used to cook for her, using readily available ingredients that are easier to find. If you order *gaeng som* in Thailand, it will be completely different, often made with local vegetables and fish unique to the region. This dish is my way of blending traditional flavours with what's available around me.

1 litre/4 cups chicken stock (homemade or from stock cubes)
100 g/3½ oz. fine green beans, cut into bite-sized pieces
100 g/3½ oz. pak choi/boy choy, cut into bite-sized pieces
1 carrot, cut into bite-sized pieces
¼ of a Savoy cabbage, roughly chopped
1 courgette/zucchini, cut into 1-cm/½-inch slices
100 g/3½ oz. cherry tomatoes, halved
300 g/10½ oz. salmon, cut into bite-sized pieces
4 tablespoons tamarind paste
4 tablespoons fish sauce
1 large red chilli/chile, thinly sliced
sticky rice or steamed jasmine rice, to serve (optional)

CHILLI PASTE
6 large hot red chillies/chiles, chopped
thumb-size piece of galangal, chopped
1 lemongrass stalk
2 small shallots, chopped
4 garlic cloves
1 tablespoon shrimp paste
1 teaspoon salt
1 teaspoon ground turmeric

SERVES 2–3

First, make the chilli paste. Add the red chilies, galangal, lemongrass, shallots, garlic, shrimp paste, salt and turmeric to a blender or mortar and pestle. Blend or pound into a smooth paste. Add a small amount of water if needed to help blend, then set aside.

In a large saucepan, bring the chicken stock to a gentle boil over a medium heat. Stir in the prepared chilli paste and cook for 3–5 minutes to release its aroma and infuse the broth.

Add the fine green beans, pak choi, carrot, cabbage, courgette and cherry tomatoes to the pan. Simmer for 15–20 minutes, or until the vegetables are tender but not mushy.

Gently add the salmon pieces to the pan and cook for about 4–5 minutes, or until the salmon is just cooked through. Take care when stirring to prevent the fish from breaking apart. Stir in the tamarind paste, fish sauce and sliced red chilli.

Taste and adjust the seasoning by adding more tamarind paste for tanginess or fish sauce for saltiness as needed.

Ladle the hot soup into deep bowls, ensuring each portion has a good mix of vegetables and salmon. Serve immediately while hot with sticky rice or steamed jasmine rice, if liked.

Curries
แกงสูตรต้นตำรับ

Experience the heart and soul of Thai
cuisine through these cornerstone curries.

ข้าวซอย
KHAO SOI

Chicken noodle curry

Khao soi was recently voted the best soup in the world! Inspired by its popularity, I've opened a restaurant focusing on this northern Thai dish, offering a variety of creative toppings on the menu.

400 g/14 oz. chicken breasts
5 tablespoons vegetable oil, plus extra for drizzling
2 tablespoons mild curry powder
½ teaspoon salt
1 teaspoon dried parsley
500 ml/2 cups chicken stock
400 ml/14 fl oz. coconut milk
60 ml/¼ cup tamarind juice
3 tablespoons fish sauce
4 tablespoons palm sugar (or brown sugar)
250 g/9 oz. egg noodles

CHILLI PASTE
20 medium dried red chillies/chiles
3 garlic cloves
1 small shallot, chopped
handful of coriander/cilantro stalks, chopped (keep the leaves)
1 tablespoon curry powder
1 lemongrass stalk, finely chopped
grated zest of 1 lime
½ a thumb-sized piece of galangal, chopped (or use fresh ginger)
½ teaspoon each cumin seeds and coriander seeds, toasted in a pan for 1–2 minutes
1 teaspoon shrimp paste (optional)

GARNISH
handful of beansprouts, washed
chopped coriander/cilantro leaves
sliced spring onions/scallions
sliced red chilli/chile
lime wedges

SERVES 2

Preheat the oven to 220°C/200°C fan/425°F/Gas 7.

Drizzle the chicken breasts with a little vegetable oil. Season with the curry powder, salt and dried parsley, then gently rub into the meat.

Heat 2 tablespoons of the vegetable oil in a frying pan/skillet over a medium-high heat. Sear the chicken breasts for 2 minutes on each side until golden brown, flipping occasionally to prevent burning. Transfer the chicken to a baking sheet and bake for 13–15 minutes. Once cooked, let them rest for 5 minutes before slicing thinly. Set aside.

Meanwhile, prepare the chilli paste. Boil the dried red chillies in a saucepan with 300 ml/1¼ cups water for 10 minutes, or until softened. Drain the softened chillies, keeping the cooking water for later. Place the chillies in a blender along with the garlic, shallot, coriander stalks, curry powder, lemongrass, lime zest, galangal, cumin seeds, coriander seeds and shrimp paste (if using). Begin blending, adding 2 tablespoons of the reserved cooking water at a time to help achieve a smooth consistency. Continue blending for a few minutes until the mixture becomes a smooth paste, adjusting the liquid as needed.

In a medium saucepan, heat the remaining 3 tablespoons vegetable oil over a medium-high heat. Add the chilli paste and stir regularly to prevent burning. Once fragrant, pour in the chicken stock and stir to combine, then add the coconut milk. Season the soup with the tamarind juice, fish sauce and palm sugar. Adjust to taste, then let it simmer for 10 minutes before turning off the heat.

Bring a small saucepan of water to the boil. Add the egg noodles and cook for 5–7 minutes. Drain the noodles and toss them with a little vegetable oil to prevent sticking.

Divide the noodles between deep bowls and top with the sliced chicken and beansprouts. Ladle the hot curry soup over the noodles, then garnish with coriander, spring onions, sliced chillies and lime wedges.

แกงมัสมั่นใส่แกะ
GAENG MASSAMAN SAI KAE

Massaman lamb curry

Massaman curry is a well-known dish in Thailand, traditionally made with chicken or beef. However, after moving to the UK, I noticed how much people here love lamb, so I decided to create my own version using lamb instead. It quickly became the best-selling curry at my restaurant! This dish is slow-cooked in a rich coconut milk base, infused with warm spices like cinnamon and star anise with a touch of mild chilli. The result is a comforting yet incredibly delicious curry that's packed with deep, aromatic flavours. It's the perfect balance of creamy, mildly spiced goodness that warms you from the inside out – ideal for anyone looking for a hearty and satisfying meal.

4 tablespoons vegetable oil
500 g/1 lb 2 oz. diced lamb shoulder
500 ml/2 cups chicken stock
2 bay leaves
2 cinnamon sticks
2 star anise
400 ml/14 fl oz. coconut milk
1 tablespoon tamarind paste
3 tablespoons fish sauce
2 tablespoons brown sugar
2 onions, cut into bite-sized pieces
2 potatoes, cut into bite-sized pieces
4 tablespoons roasted peanuts (see page 47)
steamed jasmine rice or roti, to serve

CHILLI PASTE
6 medium dried red chillies/chiles (soaked in hot water for 10–15 minutes)
1 lemongrass stalk, chopped
2 small shallots, chopped
3 garlic cloves, chopped
½ a thumb-sized piece of galangal, chopped
½ teaspoon ground cumin
1 teaspoon ground coriander
½ teaspoon ground cinnamon
4–6 tablespoons hot water

GARNISH
sliced red chilli
chopped coriander/cilantro leaves

SERVES 2–3

First, prepare the chilli paste. In a blender, add the soaked chillies, chopped lemongrass, shallots, garlic, galangal, ground cumin, coriander and cinnamon. Blend with the hot water to form a smooth paste. Set aside until needed.

In a large saucepan, heat the vegetable oil over a medium heat. Add the chilli paste and cook for 3–5 minutes until fragrant.

Add the diced lamb and sear until lightly browned on all sides. Pour in the chicken stock, then add the bay leaves, cinnamon sticks and star anise. Let it simmer for 1–1½ hours until the lamb is tender.

Once the lamb is cooked, add the coconut milk, tamarind paste, fish sauce, brown sugar, onions, potatoes and roasted peanuts. Stir well and cook for a further 20 minutes, or until the vegetables are soft and the curry has thickened.

Garnish with sliced red chilli and coriander leaves before serving with steamed jasmine rice or roti.

แกงคั่วสับปะรด
GAENG KUA SAPPAROD

Beef & pineapple curry

A sweet and savoury dish of tender beef and juicy pineapple simmered in a creamy red curry. *Gaeng kua sapparod* reminds me of my school days when I'd always choose a sweet and savoury dish for lunch. I've always loved the addition of fruity flavours in savoury curries, and this one was a favourite. The sweetness of the pineapple mixed with the rich, creamy curry made it stand out from other dishes. It felt special, like a little treat in the middle of the day. Even now, whenever I make this dish, it brings back memories of those simple, happy school lunches.

3 tablespoons vegetable oil
200 g/7 oz. sirloin steak, thinly sliced
½ a medium pineapple, cut into bite-sized pieces
200 ml/scant 1 cup beef stock
400 ml/14 fl oz. coconut milk (at least 65% fat content)
4 makrut lime leaves, torn
3 tablespoons fish sauce
2 tablespoons tamarind paste
3 tablespoons brown sugar
3 sprigs of Thai basil leaves
1 large red chilli/chile, cut into long thin slices
steamed jasmine rice, to serve

CHILLI PASTE
6 large hot red chillies/chiles, chopped
3 garlic cloves, chopped
2 small shallots, chopped
1 lemongrass stalk, chopped
a thumb-size piece of fresh ginger, chopped
1 teaspoon shrimp paste
1 teaspoon salt

GARNISH
chopped coriander/cilantro leaves
2–3 spring onions/scallions, chopped
Thai basil leaves

SERVES 3–4

First, prepare the chilli paste. In a blender or mortar and pestle, combine the red chillies, garlic, shallots, lemongrass, ginger, shrimp paste and salt. Blend or pound to form a smooth paste. Set aside until needed.

Heat the vegetable oil in a large saucepan over a medium heat. Add the sliced steak and cook for 1–2 minutes until just browned. Remove the steak and set aside.

In the same pan, add the chilli paste and sauté for 3–5 minutes until fragrant. Stir in the pineapple pieces and cook for a further minute. Pour in the beef stock and coconut milk, then add the lime leaves. Gently simmer for 20–25 minutes until the pineapple softens.

Return the cooked steak to the pan and season with fish sauce, tamarind paste and brown sugar. Stir well. Adjust the seasoning to taste, balancing the sweet, sour, salty and spicy flavours. Add the Thai basil leaves and red chilli. Simmer for 2 minutes.

Serve the curry immediately while hot, garnished with chopped coriander, spring onions and Thai basil leaves, alongside some steamed jasmine rice.

COOKING TIP Shrimp paste is a traditional Thai ingredient with a strong flavour and smell. We use it in almost everything in our cuisine. It gives a deep umami taste. Some dishes I cook at home even include fermented fish, which has an even stronger smell and flavour than shrimp paste. Using shrimp paste is really up to your own preference though – if you're not a fan, feel free to reduce the amount.

แกงเขียวหวานไก่
GAENG KEOW WAN GAI

Thai green chicken curry

Who doesn't love a good Thai green curry? It's a dish that has won hearts all over the world, but I have to admit, I've seen some versions that make me raise an eyebrow – especially the greyish-looking ones! I created this recipe to share with everyone who loves an authentic, vibrant green Thai curry made with a proper homemade chilli paste. In Thailand, we traditionally use chilli leaves to achieve that beautiful green colour, but since fresh chilli leaves aren't commonly found elsewhere, I've come up with a great substitute – coriander and Thai basil leaves. They not only give the curry a vibrant green hue but also add a fragrant, fresh flavour that makes this dish truly delicious.

This recipe is my way of bringing a taste of Thailand to your kitchen, with rich, creamy coconut milk and the perfect balance of spice and aromatics.

3 tablespoons vegetable oil
400 ml/14 fl oz. coconut milk
300 g/10½ oz. chicken breast, thinly sliced
2 chicken stock cubes, crumbled
2 courgettes/zucchini, cut into bite-sized pieces
1 green (bell) pepper, cut into bite-sized pieces
45 g/3 tablespoons fish sauce
4 tablespoons brown sugar
3 sprigs of Thai basil leaves
steamed jasmine rice, to serve

CHILLI PASTE
6 large green chillies/chiles (jalapeños are great for this), chopped
1 teaspoon shrimp paste
1 lemongrass stalk, chopped
3 garlic cloves, chopped
thumb-size piece of galangal
½ a handful of coriander/cilantro leaves
½ a handful of basil leaves
1 teaspoon ground cumin
1 teaspoon white peppercorns (or ½ teaspoon black peppercorns)
1 teaspoon salt

SERVES 2

First, prepare the chilli paste. In a blender or mortar and pestle, combine the green chillies, shrimp paste, lemongrass, garlic, galangal, coriander, basil leaves, cumin, white peppercorns and salt. Blend or pound to a smooth paste. Set aside until needed.

In a large saucepan, heat the oil over a medium heat. Add the chilli paste and sauté for 3–5 minutes until fragrant. Pour in the coconut milk and stir well, allowing the flavours to blend.

Add the chicken and cook for 5–7 minutes until it starts to turn white. Pour in 500 ml/2 cups water and add the crumbled stock cubes. Bring to a gentle boil and let it simmer for 10 minutes.

Stir in the courgettes and green pepper, cooking for 5 minutes, or until they are tender but still vibrant.

Season with fish sauce and brown sugar, stirring well to balance the flavours. Turn off the heat and stir in the Thai basil leaves for a fresh, fragrant finish. Serve the curry immediately while hot with steamed jasmine rice.

แกงป่าซาวมอล
GAENG PA SALMON

Salmon jungle curry

Gaeng pa, also known as jungle curry, originally comes from Southern Thailand, but it's so popular that every household across the country knows how to cook it. This dish is loved for its bold, spicy flavours and is a healthy, low-calorie option that's packed with nutritious ingredients. Thai people have a deep love for hot and spicy food, and this dish ticks all the boxes. Since moving to the UK, I've recreated this recipe using local vegetables that are easy to find in supermarkets, while still maintaining the distinctive flavours that I miss from Thailand. It's the perfect dish for anyone looking for something healthy, flavourful and truly authentic, with a little twist to suit life away from Thailand.

3 tablespoons vegetable oil
1 litre/4 cups vegetable stock
200 g/7 oz. butternut squash, peeled and cut into bite-sized pieces
100 g/3½ oz. fine green beans, cut into bite-sized pieces
2 large red (bell) peppers, cut into bite-sized pieces
1 courgette/zucchini, sliced
100 g/3½ oz. baby corn, cut into bite-sized pieces
100 g/3½ oz. pak choi/bok choy, cut into 2.5-cm/1-inch pieces
200 g/7 oz. salmon, cut into bite-sized pieces
4 tablespoons fish sauce
3 sprigs of Thai basil leaves, plus extra to garnish
steamed jasmine rice, to serve

CHILLI PASTE
6 large hot red chillies/chiles, chopped
2 stalks of Chinese key root (or a thumb-sized piece of fresh ginger), chopped
1 lemongrass stalk, chopped
2 small shallots, chopped
4 garlic cloves, chopped
2 teaspoons shrimp paste (see page 96)
1 teaspoon salt
1 teaspoon cumin seeds

SERVES 2–3

First, prepare the chilli paste. In a blender or mortar and pestle, combine the chopped red chillies, Chinese key root (or fresh ginger), lemongrass, shallots, garlic, shrimp paste, salt and cumin seeds. Blend or pound to form a smooth paste. Set aside until needed.

In a large saucepan, heat the vegetable oil over a medium heat. Add the chilli paste and sauté for 3–5 minutes until fragrant.

Pour in the vegetable stock and bring it to a gentle boil. Let it simmer for 5 minutes to allow the flavours to infuse.

As it takes longer to soften, add the butternut squash first and cook for about 5 minutes. Next, add the green beans, red peppers, courgette, baby corn and pak choi. Simmer for a further 10 minutes or until all the vegetables are tender.

Gently add the salmon pieces and cook for a further 5 minutes, ensuring they are cooked through but still tender.

Stir in the fish sauce and Thai basil leaves, then let the curry simmer for another minute. Turn off the heat.

Serve the curry while hot with steamed jasmine rice.

GAENG SOM (SEAFOOD)

Mixed seafood sour curry

Gaeng som, also known as Southern Thai sour curry, is quite similar to *Gaeng pa* (jungle curry, see page 100), but with an added tangy twist from tamarind. Originating from the south of Thailand, it's a dish packed with bold flavours and plenty of fresh vegetables, making it one of my personal favourites.

As someone who loves eating vegetables, this dish is perfect – it's light, spicy and full of vibrant, healthy ingredients. The sourness from the tamarind balances beautifully with the heat from the chillies, creating a flavourful broth that's both comforting and refreshing. Whether you enjoy it with seafood or just vegetables, *Gaeng som* is a delicious, guilt-free meal that I could eat any day of the week.

1 litre/4 cups chicken stock
1 carrot, cut into bite-sized pieces
100 g/3½ oz. fine green beans, cut into bite-sized pieces
100 g/3½ oz. pak choi/bok choy, cut into bite-sized pieces
¼ of a Savoy cabbage, roughly chopped
1 courgette/zucchini, sliced
100 g/3½ oz. cherry tomatoes, halved
4 tablespoons tamarind paste
4 tablespoons fish sauce
300 g/10½ oz. mixed seafood (such as squid rings, prawns/shrimp, mussels), cut into bite-sized pieces
1 large red chilli/chile, thinly sliced
steamed jasmine rice, to serve (optional)

CHILLI PASTE
6 large hot red chillies/chiles, chopped
thumb-sized piece of galangal, chopped
1 lemongrass stalk, chopped
2 small shallots, chopped
4 garlic cloves, chopped
1 teaspoon shrimp paste (see page 96)
1 teaspoon salt
1 teaspoon ground turmeric

SERVES 2–3

First, prepare the chilli paste. In a blender or mortar and pestle, combine the chopped red chillies, galangal, lemongrass, shallots, garlic, shrimp paste, salt and turmeric. Blend or pound to form a smooth paste. Set aside until needed.

In a large saucepan, bring the chicken stock to a gentle boil over a medium heat. Add the chilli paste and stir well. Let it simmer for about 5 minutes to allow the flavours to blend.

Add the carrot and cook for 5 minutes, followed by the green beans, pak choi, cabbage, courgette and cherry tomatoes. Simmer the vegetables for about 10 minutes or until they start to soften. Stir in the tamarind paste and fish sauce, adjusting to taste if needed.

Gently add the mixed seafood and cook for a further 5 minutes, or until the seafood is cooked through and tender. Turn off the heat and add the thinly sliced red chilli for an extra kick of spice.

Serve the curry immediately while hot, either on its own or with steamed jasmine rice.

GAENG PA PAK

Vegetable jungle curry

Gaeng pa pak is another one of my mum's favourites. Similar to Gaeng som salmon but without the tamarind or sourness, this dish is all about bold, spicy and earthy flavours. It's even spicier than gaeng som, which suits my mum perfectly since she loves dishes with intense heat. Originally from the south of Thailand, where spicy food is a way of life, Gaeng pa pak showcases the region's love for vibrant flavours and fresh local vegetables. Cooking it always reminds me of how much my mum enjoys this fiery, comforting dish, and it's a great way to bring a taste of southern Thailand to any table.

3 tablespoons vegetable oil
1 litre/4 cups vegetable stock
200 g/7 oz. aubergines/eggplant, cut into bite-sized pieces
100 g/3½ oz. fine green beans, cut into bite-sized pieces
2 large red (bell) peppers, cut into bite-sized pieces
1 courgette/zucchini, sliced
100 g/3½ oz. baby corn, cut into bite-sized pieces
200 g/7 oz. butternut squash, peeled and cut into bite-sized pieces
100 g/3½ oz. pak choi/bok choy, cut into 2.5-cm/1-inch pieces
4 tablespoons fish sauce
3 sprigs of hai basil leaves
steamed jasmine rice, to serve (optional)

CHILLI PASTE
6 large hot red chillies/chiles, chopped
2 stalks of Chinese key root (or a thumb-sized piece of fresh ginger), chopped
1 lemongrass stalk, chopped
2 small shallots, chopped
4 garlic cloves, chopped
2 teaspoons shrimp paste (see page 96)
1 teaspoon salt
1 teaspoon cumin seeds

SERVES 3–4

First, prepare the chilli paste. In a blender or mortar and pestle, combine the red chillies, Chinese key root (or fresh ginger), lemongrass, shallots, garlic, shrimp paste, salt and cumin seeds. Blend or pound to form a smooth paste. Set aside until needed.

Heat the vegetable oil in a large saucepan over a medium heat. Add the chilli paste and sauté for 3–5 minutes until fragrant.

Pour in the vegetable stock and bring to a gentle boil.

As it takes longer to soften, add the butternut squash to the pan first and cook for about 5 minutes. Next, add the aubergines, green beans, red peppers, courgette and baby corn. Simmer for a further 10–15 minutes, or until all the vegetables are tender. Stir in the pak choi and cook for a further 2 minutes.

Season the curry with fish sauce and stir in the Thai basil leaves. Taste and adjust the seasoning with fish sauce and ground black pepper as preferred.

Serve the curry immediately while hot, either on its own or with steamed jasmine rice.

GAENG KHANOON

Jackfruit Thai curry

This is a dish I grew up eating all the time. At the back of my house, we had three big jackfruit trees (*khanoon*), which gave us fruit all year round. The young jackfruit was perfect for savoury dishes like this one, while the ripe fruit was great to eat on its own or to use in desserts. I was so surprised and happy when I saw a can of young jackfruit in our local supermarket one day. It's exciting to see how this ingredient has become popular, especially in plant-based dishes.

This dish is also an important part of Thai celebrations and is often cooked for events like opening a new shop, starting a business or even weddings. The name *khanoon* in Thai also suggests support and success, so many people believe cooking it brings good luck and prosperity – ideal for marking special occasions.

2 tablespoons vegetable oil
200 g/7 oz. pork belly, thinly sliced (or you can use chicken, fish, beef or tofu)
1 litre/4 cups chicken stock
2 cans of 400-g/14-oz. young jackfruit, drained and chopped into bite-sized pieces
100 g/3½ oz. cherry tomatoes, halved
4 tablespoons fish sauce
3 tablespoons tamarind juice
2 teaspoons salt
4 coriander/cilantro sprigs, coarsely chopped
4 spring onions/scallions, coarsely chopped
sticky rice or boiled rice, to serve (optional)

CHILLI PASTE
10–15 medium dried red chillies/chiles (depending on your spice preferences)
3 garlic cloves, chopped
2 small shallots, chopped
1 teaspoon shrimp paste (optional)

SERVES 2

First, prepare the chilli paste. Place the dried red chillies in a saucepan filled with 300 ml/1¼ cups water, then boil for 10 minutes, or until softened. Drain the softened chillies, keeping the cooking water for later.

Place the chillies in a blender along with the garlic, shallots and shrimp paste (if using). Begin blending, adding 2 tablespoons of the reserved cooking water at a time to achieve a smooth consistency. Continue blending for a few minutes until the mixture becomes a smooth paste, adjusting the liquid as needed.

In a large saucepan, heat the vegetable oil over a medium-high heat. Add the chilli paste and cook for 2 minutes, stirring continuously. Add the sliced pork belly and continue cooking over medium heat for 5 minutes, or until the pork is fully cooked.

Pour in the chicken stock and bring it to the boil. Add the young jackfruit and cherry tomatoes, stirring regularly to prevent sticking. Cover with a lid, reduce the heat and let it simmer for 10–15 minutes, or until the young jackfruit becomes tender.

Season with the fish sauce, tamarind juice and salt, adjusting to taste. Finally, stir in the chopped coriander and spring onions.

Serve the curry immediately while hot. Traditionally, this curry is served with sticky rice, although regular boiled rice is equally delicious.

แกงเผ็ดใส่ขาเป็ดนุ่ม
GAENG PED SAI KHA PED NOOM

Duck leg confit with red curry

In Thailand, duck is a beloved meat, often enjoyed as roasted duck with Chinese-style sauces. However, when my local farm started supplying us with fresh duck legs, I wanted to create something unique that highlights their rich, tender taste. That's how this dish came to life – combining the slow, gentle cooking of confit, which makes the duck incredibly tender, with the bold, aromatic flavours of Thai red curry. It's a best-seller at my restaurant and a dish that truly showcases the harmony between East and West.

500 g/1 lb 2 oz. duck legs
2 x 400 ml/14 oz. cans of coconut milk
1 lemongrass stalk, bruised
3 tablespoons vegetable oil
100 g/3½ oz. cherry tomatoes, halved
1 tablespoon tamarind paste
3 tablespoons brown sugar
2 tablespoons fish sauce
steamed jasmine rice, to serve (optional)

CHILLI PASTE
6 large dried red chillies/chiles, boiled in hot water for 10–15 minutes until softened
6 medium dried red chillies/chiles, boiled in hot water for 10–15 minutes until softened
thumb-sized piece of galangal, chopped
1 lemongrass stalk, chopped
2 small shallots, chopped
4 garlic cloves, chopped
1 teaspoon shrimp paste (see page 96)
½ teaspoon salt
½ teaspoon ground cumin powder
½ teaspoon ground coriander

GARNISH
1 large red chilli/chile, cut into long thin slices
2–3 sprigs of Thai basil leaves

SERVES 2–3

In a large saucepan, combine the duck legs, one of the cans of coconut milk, bruised lemongrass stalk and 500 ml/2 cups water. Bring to a gentle boil over a medium heat, then reduce to low and let it simmer for 1½–2 hours, or until the duck legs are tender and the meat easily pulls away from the bone. Remove the duck legs from the pan and set aside until later.

Meanwhile, prepare the chilli paste. In a blender or mortar and pestle, combine the soaked chillies, galangal, lemongrass, shallots, garlic, shrimp paste, salt, cumin and coriander. Blend or pound to form a smooth paste. Set aside until needed.

In a separate pan, heat the vegetable oil over medium heat. Add the chilli paste and sauté for 3–5 minutes until fragrant.

Pour in the remaining can of coconut milk and stir well. Add the cherry tomatoes, tamarind paste, brown sugar and fish sauce. Let it simmer for 10 minutes, allowing the flavours to blend.

Return the cooked duck legs to the pan with the curry sauce and simmer for a further 10–15 minutes, ensuring the meat absorbs the flavours.

Serve the curry immediately while hot, garnished with sliced red chilli and Thai basil leaves , either on its own or with steamed jasmine rice.

COOKING TIP There is a reason that I use different sized dried chillies in the chilli paste. The large dried chillies don't have much heat, but they help give the curry a deep red colour. The medium chillies are the ones that add the heat. So to get the right balance of colour and spice, I use both.

GAENG FAK THONG

Northern Thai pumpkin curry

A creamy and mild curry made with pumpkin or butternut squash, coconut milk and a fragrant mix of spices like cinnamon, nutmeg and coriander. Northern Thai pumpkin curry always takes me back to the days when we had pumpkin plants growing in the backyard. The leaves were so big, I remember thinking they were larger than my head! The pumpkins were green on the outside but bright orange on the inside. Now, living away from home, I tweak the recipe to use butternut squash, which is easier to find but still tastes just as good. My mum told me this was my grandma's favourite dish. I was too young to remember her since she passed away when I was little, but every time I cook it, I imagine sharing it with her, hoping she would have loved it as much as I do.

1 litre/4 cups vegetable stock

1 butternut squash, peeled and cut into bite-sized pieces (around 500–600 g/1 lb 2 oz.–1 lb 5 oz.)

100 g/3½ oz. fine green beans, cut into bite-sized pieces

100 g/3½ oz. baby corn, cut into bite-sized pieces

2 onions, cut into bite-sized pieces

1 courgette/zucchini, sliced

4 tablespoons fish sauce

small handful of dill, roughly chopped, plus extra to garnish

steamed jasmine rice, to serve (optional)

CHILLI PASTE

2 large red hot chillies/chiles, chopped

2 large green chillies/chiles (green jalapeños can also be used)

4 garlic cloves, chopped

2 small shallots, chopped

2 teaspoons shrimp paste (see page 96)

SERVES 3–4

First, prepare the chilli paste. In a blender or mortar and pestle, combine the red chillies, green chillies, garlic, shallots and shrimp paste. Blend or pound to form a smooth paste. Set aside until needed.

Heat a large saucepan over a medium heat. Add the chilli paste and sauté for 3–5 minutes until fragrant.

Pour in the vegetable stock and bring to a gentle boil. Add the butternut squash to the pan and simmer for 15–20 minutes.

Stir in the green beans, baby corn, onions and courgette. Simmer for a further 10–12 minutes, or until all the vegetables are tender.

Season the curry with fish sauce and stir in the chopped dill. Taste and adjust the seasoning with fish sauce or ground black pepper if needed.

Serve the curry immediately while hot garnished with extra dill if liked, either on its own or with steamed jasmine rice.

COOKING TIP this dish can easily be made vegetarian or vegan by using vegan fish sauce or soy sauce and using white miso paste instead of shrimp paste.

Stir-fries
ของผัด

From the wok to the plate – fresh and
quick-cooking recipes for every day.

KRAPOW GAI

Stir-fried chicken with holy basil

This dish takes me back to my first attempts at cooking during food tech classes at school. It was one of the first dishes I ever made, and although it wasn't perfect at the time, it quickly became a favourite. At home, we had a holy basil plant growing in the back yard, along with chillies/chiles and other herbs, so I'd always collect fresh ingredients to use. Those fresh flavours made the dish extra special to me, and now I want to share that authentic taste with you.

3 tablespoons vegetable oil
2 garlic cloves, crushed
2 red chillies/chiles, cut into long thin slices
1 red onion, thinly sliced
200 g/7 oz. minced/ground chicken
1 tablespoon oyster sauce
1 tablespoon light soy sauce
1 tablespoon brown sugar
1 teaspoon dark soy sauce
handful of holy basil leaves

TO SERVE (OPTIONAL)
boiled or steamed jasmine rice
2 fried eggs

SERVES 2

Heat the vegetable oil in a large pan or wok over a medium-high heat. Add the garlic, red chillies and red onion and stir-fry for 2–3 minutes until the onion softens.

Add the chicken and cook, stirring continuously, breaking up any clumps with a wooden spoon. Season with the oyster sauce, light soy sauce, brown sugar and dark soy sauce. Mix well to coat the meat evenly. Finally, toss in a handful of holy basil leaves, stir briefly and turn off the heat.

Serve the chicken with boiled or steamed jasmine rice topped with a fried egg, if preferred.

COOKING TIP Holy basil is different from Thai basil and regular basil as it has a more peppery, clove flavour.

ผัดฉ่า
PAD CHA

Stir-fried mixed seafood

A spicy seafood stir-fry cooked with chillies/chiles, garlic, ginger and fragrant Thai herbs. This dish is intensely aromatic and bursting with bold flavours.

Pad cha wasn't something I'd usually order in Thailand – there were just so many options to choose from! But here in England, it has become my go-to takeaway. There's something about its bold, spicy flavours that always hits the spot. Still, as much as I love ordering it, sometimes it's just not the same as making it yourself. That's why I created this recipe. It's quick, simple, and packed with flavour. Best of all, it can be done in less than 20 minutes, making it the perfect dinner after a busy day.

3 tablespoons vegetable oil
2 large hot red chillies/chiles, finely chopped
3 garlic cloves, crushed/minced
1 onion, sliced
200 g/7 oz. mixed seafood (such as prawns.shrimp, squid rings, mussels)
100 g/3½ oz. mangetout
100 g/3½ oz. baby corn, cut into bite-sized pieces
2 Chinese key roots (or a thumb-sized piece of fresh ginger, thinly sliced into strips)
3 tablespoons oyster sauce
1 tablespoon dark soy sauce
1 tablespoon brown sugar
½ teaspoon ground white pepper
small handful of Thai basil
steamed jasmine rice, to serve (optional)

SERVES 2

Heat the vegetable oil in a large pan or wok over a medium-high heat. Add the red chillies and garlic and sauté for 1–2 minutes until fragrant. Add the sliced onion and stir-fry for a further 2 minutes until slightly softened.

Stir in the mixed seafood and cook for 2–3 minutes until it starts to turn opaque. Add the mangetout, baby corn and Chinese key roots (or fresh ginger). Stir-fry for a further 2 minutes.

Pour in the oyster sauce, dark soy sauce, brown sugar and 200 ml/scant 1 cup water. Stir well to combine and bring the mixture to a simmer. Season with the white pepper, then stir in the Thai basil leaves. Cook for 1 minute until the basil is fragrant and the seafood is fully cooked.

Serve the stir-fry immediately while hot, either on its own or with steamed jasmine rice.

COOKING TIP Chinese key roots can be quite difficult to find unless you visit a speciality Asian supermarket, so the best substitute is fresh ginger.

PAD THAI GOONG

Classic pad Thai with king prawns

This is one of the most well-known Thai dishes. Over the years, I've tried countless versions both inside and outside of Thailand, but not everyone gets it right. So, what makes a good *Pad Thai*? It's all about balance and technique. The noodles should be perfectly cooked – tender but not overdone – and evenly coated with the rich, flavourful *Pad Thai* sauce. When done right, it's an unforgettable dish that brings together sweet, savoury and tangy flavours in every bite. Here is my version...

2 tablespoons vegetable oil
2 garlic cloves, crushed
100 g/3½ oz. king prawns/ jumbo shrimp, peeled and deveined
2 large/US extra-large eggs
200 g/7 oz. rice stick noodles, soaked in warm water for 30 minutes
handful of beansprouts
3 spring onions/scallions, cut into long thin slices
1 teaspoon dried chilli/hot red pepper flakes

PAD THAI SAUCE
2 tablespoons vegetable oil
3 garlic cloves, crushed/minced
1 small shallot, very finely chopped
2 tablespoons tomato ketchup
2 tablespoons tamarind juice (see cooking tip)
2 tablespoons oyster sauce
2 tablespoons light soy sauce
6 tablespoons palm sugar (or brown sugar)
1 tablespoon fish sauce

GARNISH
2 tablespoons coarsely chopped roasted peanuts (see page 47, optional)
3–4 coriander/cilantro leaves
sliced red chillies/chiles
lime wedges

SERVES 2

First, prepare the pad Thai sauce. Heat the vegetable oil in a saucepan over a low heat. Add the garlic and shallots and gently cook for 2 minutes until softened. Stir in the tomato ketchup, tamarind juice, oyster sauce, light soy sauce, palm sugar and fish sauce. Simmer for 5 minutes, stirring continuously, then set aside until needed.

Heat the vegetable oil in a large pan or wok over a medium-high heat. Add the garlic and prawns and cook for 2–4 minutes until the prawns are opaque and just cooked through. Transfer the prawns to a bowl and set aside.

Using the same pan or wok, crack in the eggs and cook over a medium heat, stirring regularly to avoid burning. Return the cooked prawns to the wok, then add the soaked rice stick noodles and 3–4 tablespoons of the pad Thai sauce adjusting to taste. Stir in the beansprouts, spring onions and dried chilli, mixing well.

Transfer the pad Thai to plates and garnish with chopped peanuts (if using), coriander leaves, chilli and lime wedges.

COOKING TIP To make tamarind juice from pulp, take a small handful of tamarind pulp and place it in a bowl. Pour just enough warm water over the pulp to cover it and let it soak for about 10–15 minutes to soften. Using your hands or a spoon, gently mash and squeeze the pulp to extract the tamarind essence into the water. Strain the mixture through a fine-mesh sieve/strainer or cheesecloth/muslin to remove any seeds and fibres, leaving you with smooth tamarind juice.

ชิลียากิโซบะ
CHILLI YAKISOBA

Japanese stir-fried wheat noodles
with a Thai twist & homemade yakisoba sauce

Chilli yakisoba is a dish I created during my time in Japan. I remember going to a restaurant and ordering *yakisoba*, but after the first bite, I felt it needed a kick of spice. I reached for the chilli powder and chilli oil condiments on the table and, without hesitation, added almost the entire shaker – I just love my food spicy! That experience inspired me to recreate the dish with my own twist, ensuring it has the bold, fiery flavours I crave while keeping the essence of the original Japanese stir-fried noodles.

500 g/1 lb 2 oz. egg noodles
4 tablespoons vegetable oil
200 g/7 oz. chicken breast, thinly sliced
4 garlic cloves, crushed/minced
2 large hot red chillies/chiles, cut into long thin slices
¼ of a Savoy cabbage, shredded
1 carrot, thinly sliced into matchsticks or ribbons
4–5 shiitake mushrooms, sliced
100 g/3½ oz. mangetout
4 spring onions/scallions, cut into long thin slices
3 tablespoons light soy sauce
2 tablespoons dark soy sauce
2 tablespoons brown sugar
½ teaspoons ground white pepper

SERVES 2

Soak the egg noodles in warm water for 30 minutes, then drain and set aside until needed.

Heat 2 tablespoons of the vegetable oil in a large frying pan/skillet or wok over a medium-high heat. Add the chicken and stir-fry for 3–4 minutes until just cooked through. Remove from the pan and set aside.

In the same pan, add the remaining 2 tablespoons of vegetable oil. Sauté the garlic and red chillies for 1–2 minutes until fragrant.

Add the cabbage, carrot, mushrooms, mangetout and spring onions. Stir-fry for 4–5 minutes until the vegetables are tender but still crisp.

Return the chicken to the pan, then add the drained egg noodles. Toss well to combine.

In a small bowl, mix together the light soy sauce, dark soy sauce, brown sugar and white pepper. Pour the sauce over the noodles and toss everything together until evenly coated and heated through.

Serve the noodles immediately while hot.

ผัดมะเขือใส่เต้าหู้
PAD MAKEU SAI TAO HOO

Stir-fried aubergine with tofu

This dish is one of my favourites, especially during the Vegetarian Festival in Thailand. As Buddhists, we often follow a vegetarian diet from time to time to earn good karma, and this dish always brings back fond memories of those festival days. I created this recipe to capture the flavours I loved from those times. While I'm not a vegetarian, I enjoy eating plant-based dishes every now and then, and this one is always a satisfying choice. My mum, who introduced me to this dish, once told me that my version tastes even better than hers – so I knew I had to share it with everyone! Whether you're vegan or just looking for a delicious meat-free meal, this stir-fried aubergine with tofu is packed with flavour and nostalgia.

3 tablespoons vegetable oil
3 garlic cloves, crushed/minced
1 large red chilli/chile, finely chopped
200 g/7 oz. firm tofu, cut into cubes
1 large aubergine/eggplant, cut into bite-sized pieces
2 tablespoons light soy sauce
1 tablespoon dark soy sauce
1 teaspoon brown sugar
1 tablespoon fermented soy bean paste (or white miso)
½ teaspoon ground white pepper
3 sprigs of coriander/cilantro sprigs, stalks and leaves chopped
steamed jasmine rice, to serve

SERVES 2

Heat the vegetable oil in a large pan or wok over a medium heat. Add the garlic and chilli, then stir-fry for about 30 seconds until fragrant.

Add the tofu cubes and stir-fry for 3–4 minutes until lightly golden on all sides. Transfer the tofu, garlic and chilli to a bowl and set aside.

In the same pan or wok, add the aubergine and stir-fry for about 5 minutes until slightly softened. Pour in 100 ml/scant ½ cup water, cover the pan and let the aubergine cook for a further 5 minutes until tender.

Stir in the light soy sauce, dark soy sauce, brown sugar, fermented soy bean paste (or white miso) and white pepper. Mix well to coat the aubergine pieces evenly.

Return the tofu to the pan or wok and stir everything together, letting it cook for a further 2–3 minutes until the sauce thickens and coats the ingredients well. Turn off the heat and garnish with coriander.

Serve the stir-fry immediately while hot with steamed jasmine rice.

ราดหน้า
RAD NA

Stir-fried rice noodles with gravy sauce

A popular Thai noodle dish consisting of wide rice noodles smothered in a savoury gravy sauce and topped with tender slices of pork and vegetables.

This dish was a childhood favourite of mine, especially because it contains no chilli, making it a hit with kids. It's a comforting, hearty meal that reminds me of cozy, rainy Sundays when my family would gather around to enjoy a big pot of these noodles together.

4 tablespoons vegetable oil
2 large/US extra-large eggs
200 g/7 oz. Tenderstem broccoli, cut into bite-sized pieces
1 small carrot, peeled and sliced
1 litre/4 cups chicken stock
2 tablespoons light soy sauce
2 tablespoons soy bean paste (or miso paste)
4 tablespoons brown sugar
1 tablespoon dark soy sauce
1 teaspoon ground white pepper
2 tablespoons cornflour/cornstarch

MARINATED PORK
400 g/14 oz. pork shoulder, thinly sliced
2 large/US extra-large eggs
1 tablespoon oyster sauce
1 tablespoon light soy sauce
1 tablespoon vegetable oil
½ teaspoon ground white pepper

NOODLES
3 tablespoons vegetable oil
500 g/1 lb 2 oz. wide rice noodles, soaked in hot water for 10–15 minutes until softened
1 tablespoon dark soy sauce

GARNISH
lime wedges
dried chilli/hot red pepper flakes

SERVES 2–3

First, marinate the pork. In a mixing bowl, combine the pork shoulder, eggs, oyster sauce, light soy sauce, vegetable oil and ground white pepper. Mix well and leave to marinate for at least 30 minutes.

Next, prepare the noodles. Heat the vegetable oil in a large frying pan/skillet or wok over a medium-high heat. Toss in the soaked rice noodles and stir-fry for 2–3 minutes. Add the soy sauce and continue stir-frying until the noodles are evenly coated and slightly caramelized. Remove from the pan and set aside.

In the same pan, heat some vegetable oil over a medium heat. Add the marinated pork and cook for 5 minutes, or until fully cooked and slightly browned. Push the pork to one side of the pan, crack in the eggs and scramble them until just cooked. Mix them together with the pork.

Add the Tenderstem broccoli and carrot, stir-frying for 2–3 minutes until the vegetables start to soften. Pour in the chicken stock, light soy sauce, soy bean paste (or miso paste), brown sugar, dark soy sauce and white pepper. Stir well and bring to a gentle simmer.

In a small bowl, dissolve the cornflour in 300 ml/1¼ cups water, then slowly pour it into the pan while stirring continuously to thicken the gravy. Let it cook for a further 2–3 minutes until the sauce reaches a smooth, thick consistency.

Divide the stir-fried noodles between serving plates and pour the rich gravy over them. Garnish with lime wedges and serve with dried chilli flakes on the side for extra heat.

ผัดขี้เมา
PAD KEE MAO

Drunken noodles

A stir-fried noodle dish that combines wide, flat rice noodles, assorted seafood and flavourful sauces. It is a spicy and aromatic dish with a perfect balance of flavours. *Pad kee mao*, or Drunken Noodles, is a dish with a name that grabs attention. It's famously known as a hangover cure, though I can't say if that's true since I don't drink and so don't need a cure! What I do know is that it's incredibly spicy, packed with bold flavours and can leave your tongue tingling from the heat. With its fiery kick, it's a dish that wakes up your taste buds and keeps you coming back for more. Just a heads-up, if you're not a fan of super spicy food, it's best to go easy on the chilli!

200 g/7 oz. wide, flat rice noodles
4 tablespoons vegetable oil
200 g/7 oz. chicken breast, thinly sliced
4 garlic cloves, crushed/minced
2 birds eye chillies/chiles, finely chopped
2 large hot red chillies/chiles, finely chopped
3–4 chestnut mushrooms, sliced
100 g/3½ oz. baby corn, cut into bite-sized pieces
1 yellow (bell) pepper, cut into bite-sized pieces
50 g/1¾ oz. mangetout, cut into bite-sized pieces
handful of Thai basil leaves, plus extra to garnish

SAUCE
3 tablespoons oyster sauce
3 tablespoons light soy sauce
3 tablespoons hot water
1 tablespoon dark soy sauce
2 teaspoons brown sugar

SERVES 2

Soak the rice noodles in warm water for 30 minutes, then drain and set aside until needed.

Heat 2 tablespoons of vegetable oil in a large pan or wok over a medium-high heat. Add the chicken and stir-fry for 2–3 minutes until just cooked through. Remove the chicken from the pan and set aside.

In the same pan, add the remaining vegetable oil. Sauté the garlic and chillies for 1–2 minutes until fragrant. Add the mushrooms, baby corn, yellow pepper and mangetout. Stir-fry for 3–4 minutes until the vegetables are slightly tender but still crisp. Return the chicken to the pan and add the drained rice noodles. Stir well to combine.

Meanwhile, prepare the sauce. In a small bowl, mix together the oyster sauce, light soy sauce, hot water, dark soy sauce and brown sugar. Pour the sauce over the noodles and toss everything together until evenly coated and heated through.

Stir in the Thai basil leaves and cook for a further 1 minute until fragrant. Serve the noodles immediately while hot.

PAD PONG KRAREE

Yellow curry stir-fry

Pad pong kraree is a dish I always associate with the beautiful blue swimmer crabs of Thailand. Their firm, chunky meat is perfect for this rich and creamy curry. Unfortunately, it's hard to find that kind of crab here, where the meat is often flakier and better suited to other dishes. To bring this dish to life, I've created a recipe using canned chunky crab meat, which works surprisingly well. It may not be exactly the same as the fresh blue swimmer crabs from southern Thailand, but it's still delicious and brings back those flavours I love. This versatile dish can be made with crab, prawns, fish or tofu.

3 tablespoons vegetable oil
1 onion, sliced
2 celery sticks/ribs, cut into long slices
½ red (bell) pepper, sliced
½ yellow (bell) pepper, sliced
1 tablespoon mild curry powder
200 g/7 oz. canned chunky crab meat, drained
3 large/US extra-large eggs, lightly beaten
3 tablespoons oyster sauce
2 tablespoons brown sugar
100 g/scant ½ cup evaporated milk
steamed jasmine rice, to serve

GARNISH
1 large red chilli/chile, thinly sliced
chopped coriander/cilantro leaves
lime wedges

SERVES 2

Heat the vegetable oil in a large frying pan/skillet or wok over a medium heat. Add the onion and celery and sauté for 2–3 minutes until slightly softened. Add the red and yellow peppers and cook for 2 minutes. Stir in the curry powder and mix well with the vegetables until fragrant.

Add the drained crab meat and gently stir to combine, being careful not to break the meat apart too much. Pour in the lightly beaten eggs and gently stir until they start to set and coat the other ingredients.

Add the oyster sauce, brown sugar and evaporated milk. Stir well and let it simmer for 3–5 minutes until the sauce thickens slightly.

Serve the stir-fry immediately while hot, garnished with sliced red chilli, coriander leaves and lime wedges, with steamed jasmine rice.

Traditional dishes
อาหารเหนือพื้นบ้าน

The flavours of northern Thailand –
From Lanna Kingdom to your kitchen.

LARB MUANG

Northern Thai larb

Larb muang holds a lot of memories for me because it was the dish my family loved to cook every Sunday, our special gathering day. It reminds me of how families here come together for Sunday lunch. We'd prepare this dish, serving half of it raw for the adults and the other half cooked for the children. I always stuck with the cooked version, I never dared to try the raw one! After lunch, the whole family would gather around our small TV, watching boxing matches together. It wasn't just about the food; it was about spending time with family and sharing simple joys.

Made without lime juice and often seasoned with a blend of dried spices like cumin, cloves, star anise and Szechuan pepper, it can be made with pork, chicken, beef or tofu.

300 g/10½ oz. minced/ground pork
handful of coriander/cilantro leaves, chopped
2–3 spring onions/scallions, chopped
2 tablespoons fish sauce
1 pork/ham stock cube, crumbled
steamed sticky rice, jasmine rice or lettuce leaves, to serve

CHILLI MIX
2 tablespoons vegetable oil
10 medium dried red chillies/chiles
2 large dried red chillies/chiles
4 garlic cloves, chopped
2 small shallots, halved
1 teaspoon cumin seeds
2 teaspoons coriander seeds
1 teaspoon Szechuan pepper
1 teaspoon ground cinnamon
½ a thumb-sized piece of galangal, sliced
1 lemongrass stalk, sliced

CRISPY SHALLOTS & GARLIC
500 ml/2 cups vegetable oil
3 shallots, thinly sliced
1 tablespoon cornflour/cornstarch, for coating the shallots
5 garlic cloves, very thinly sliced

SERVES 2–3

First, prepare the chilli mix. Heat the vegetable oil in a frying pan/skillet over a medium heat. Add the dried chillies, garlic, shallots, cumin seeds, coriander seeds, Szechuan pepper, cinnamon, galangal and lemongrass. Sauté the ingredients for 3–5 minutes until fragrant. Remove from the heat, transfer to a blender or mortar and pestle, then blend or pound to a coarse paste. Set aside until needed.

Next, prepare the crispy shallots and garlic. Heat the vegetable oil in a small saucepan over a medium heat. Toss the shallots in the cornflour until lightly coated. Fry the shallots in the hot oil for 3–4 minutes until golden and crispy. Remove with a slotted spoon and drain on paper towels to absorb any excess oil.

Using the same oil, fry the garlic for 2–3 minutes until golden and crispy. Remove with a slotted spoon and drain on paper towels. Reserve 3 tablespoons of the garlic frying oil for later.

In a large pan or wok, heat the reserved 3 tablespoons garlic frying oil over a medium heat. Add the chilli mix and sauté for 2–3 minutes until fragrant. Add the pork and fry until browned and fully cooked, breaking up any clumps with a wooden spoon. Stir in the coriander, spring onions, fish sauce and crumbled stock cube. Mix well and cook for a further 2 minutes.

Transfer the *larb muang* to a serving plate. Garnish with crispy shallots and garlic. Serve immediately while hot with steamed sticky rice or jasmine rice or lettuce leaves, if preferred.

น้ำพริกอ่องหมู
NAM PRIK ONG MOO

Northern Thai pork chilli dip

This renowned dish, featured in my MasterChef UK 2023 final, is a tomato-based chilli dip made with minced/ground pork, tomatoes, garlic, red chillies/chiles and served with raw vegetables. This dish was my grandad's favourite. It's simple yet incredibly flavourful. When I was young, I loved watching him cook it in the kitchen. He would always adjust the spice level, making it milder so I could enjoy it too. This dish is pure comfort and also healthy because it's traditionally served with a variety of fresh vegetables, which is perfect for encouraging kids to eat their greens (something my grandad always managed to do with me). I still cook this dish regularly; it's not only delicious but also brings back wonderful memories of my childhood and the time spent with my grandad.

2 tablespoons vegetable oil
500 g/1 lb 2 oz. minced/ground pork
200 g/7 oz. cherry tomatoes, halved
4 tablespoons tamarind juice (see page 118)
4 tablespoons fish sauce
4 tablespoons palm sugar (or brown sugar)
3 sprigs of coriander/cilantro, leaves and stalks chopped
3 spring onions/scallions, chopped

CHILLI PASTE
15–20 dried red chillies/chiles
3 garlic cloves, chopped
2 small shallots, chopped
very small handful of coriander/cilantro stalks, chopped
1 teaspoon shrimp paste (optional)
2 teaspoons white miso paste

TO SERVE
fresh vegetables (little gem lettuce, cucumber, fine green beans, celery stalks/ribs) or sticky or boiled rice

SERVES 2

First, prepare the chilli paste. Boil the dried red chillies in a saucepan with 300 ml/1¼ cups water for 10 minutes or until softened. Drain the softened chillies, keeping the cooking water for later. Place the chillies in a blender along with the garlic, shallots, coriander stalks, shrimp paste (if using) and miso paste. Begin blending, adding 2 tablespoons of the reserved cooking water at a time to achieve a smooth consistency. Continue blending for a few minutes until it turns into a smooth paste, adjusting the liquid as needed.

Heat the vegetable oil in a large saucepan over a medium-high heat. Add the chilli paste and sauté for 2 minutes until fragrant. Add the pork and cook, stirring continuously to break up any clumps, for 5 minutes, or until fully cooked.

Add the cherry tomatoes and season with the tamarind juice, fish sauce and palm sugar. Let it simmer for 10 minutes, or until the tomatoes soften and the flavours have developed. Turn off the heat, then stir in the chopped coriander and spring onion for a fresh finish.

Spoon the chilli dip into a small serving bowl, then serve it with fresh vegetables for dipping or swith sticky rice or boiled rice.

COOKING TIP Traditionally, a mortar and pestle are used to make the chilli paste, but a small blender can save time.

ห่อหมกซีฟู้ด
HOR MOK SEAFOOD

Steamed seafood curry

This dish takes me back to the days when I would catch fresh catfish from the river near our home. It was always exciting to bring back the fish and turn them into something delicious. Now, I've adapted the recipe to use mixed seafood instead, but it still carries the same comforting flavours.

300 g/10½ oz. mixed seafood (such as prawns/shrimp, squid rings, mussels)
4 large/US extra-large eggs
400 ml/14 fl oz. can of coconut milk (at least 65% fat content)
1 tablespoon cornflour/cornstarch
4 makrut lime leaves, finely chopped
handful of Thai basil leaves
2 teaspoons sugar
1 tablespoon fish sauce
4–5 pieces of banana leaves
¼ of a Savoy or white cabbage, shredded
1 tablespoon cornflour/cornstarch
steamed jasmine rice, to serve

CHILLI PASTE
4 large dried red chillies/chiles
10 small dried red chillies/chiles
4 garlic cloves, chopped
2 small shallots, chopped
1 teaspoon cumin seeds
1 teaspoon coriander seeds
2 teaspoons salt
2 teaspoons shrimp paste

GARNISH
1 large red chilli/chile, thinly sliced
chopped coriander/cilantro leaves

2–3 ramekins
steamer

SERVES 2–3

First, prepare the chilli paste. Boil the dried red chillies in a saucepan with 300 ml/1¼ cups water for 30 minutes, or until softened. Drain the softened chillies. Place the chillies in a blender or mortar and pestle along with the garlic, shallots, cumin seeds, coriander seeds, salt and shrimp paste. Blend or pound to a smooth paste (use a little coconut milk to help it loosen if needed). Set aside until needed.

In a large mixing bowl, combine the chilli paste, mixed seafood, eggs, half of the coconut milk, cornflour, lime leaves, Thai basil leaves, sugar and fish sauce. Mix well until fully combined.

Cut small pieces of banana leaf and place one inside each ramekin, ensuring it covers the base and part of the sides. This will add fragrance and authenticity to the dish.

Place a layer of shredded cabbage in the bottom of each ramekin. Spoon the seafood mixture on top, filling the ramekins evenly.

In a small saucepan, mix the remaining coconut milk with the cornflour. Heat gently, while stirring, until it thickens slightly and set aside.

Place the ramekins in a steamer and steam over a medium heat for about 20–25 minutes, or until the mixture is set and cooked through. Spoon a little of the coconut sauce over the top of each ramekin for a creamy finish, then steam for a further 5 minutes.

Carefully remove the ramekins from the steamer. Garnish with sliced red chilli and chopped coriander leaves. Let the ramekins of curry stand for 5–10 minutes before serving alongside some steamed jasmine rice.

GAENG OM GAI

Herbal broth with chicken

Gaeng om gai is a rare treat, often cooked for special occasions like birthdays or family gatherings. Growing up, I remember how every house in my village had a vegetable garden or raised chickens for food. Occasionally, we would prepare this dish by using a chicken from our own backyard, making it even more special. I never killed the chickens myself; that was always the responsibility of my grandad or uncle. Cooking *Gaeng om gai* now brings back those memories of simple living and the rare moments of indulgence that made this dish feel so special.

2 chicken stock cubes, crumbled
2 lemongrass stalks, cut into long slices
thumb-sized piece of galangal, sliced
4 makrut lime leaves, torn
1 onion, sliced
8–10 dried red chillies/chiles
500 g/1 lb 2 oz. chicken thighs, bone removed, cut into bite-sized pieces
3 tablespoons lime juice
1 teaspoon salt
3 tablespoons fish sauce
2 tablespoons light soy sauce
handful of coriander/cilantro leaves, chopped
3–4 spring onions/scallions, chopped
steamed jasmine rice, to serve (optional)

SERVES 2–3

In a large saucepan, bring 1 litre/4 cups water to the boil. Add the chicken stock cubes, lemongrass, galangal, lime leaves and onion and simmer for 5–7 minutes, allowing the flavours to develop.

Toast the dried red chillies in a dry frying pan/skillet until fragrant, then crush them in a mortar and pestle. Add the crushed chillies to the saucepan with the stock and simmer for a further 2 minutes.

Add the chicken thighs to the saucepan and cook for 10–12 minutes, or until the chicken is fully cooked and tender.

Stir in the lime juice, salt, fish sauce and light soy sauce. Taste and adjust the seasoning if needed to balance the salty, sour and spicy flavours.

Remove the pan from the heat and stir in the chopped coriander and spring onions. Serve the broth immediately while hot, either on its own or with steamed jasmine rice.

COOKING TIP I normally used chicken thighs or drumsticks with the bone in. I find the meat is so juicy and has a natural sweetness to it. You can use chicken breasts, if preferred, but make sure you don't overcook them, otherwise the meat will become dry and chewy.

TAM KANOON

Spicy jackfruit & pork

Tam kanoon is one of my all-time favourite dishes. Back in Thailand, whenever we were unsure what to cook for dinner, I would head to the back of our garden to check if we had any young jackfruits growing on our trees. We were lucky to have three jackfruit trees, which meant we had a steady supply of fruit all year round.

This dish is simple yet delicious, embodying the heart of Northern Thai cuisine – humble, comforting and packed with flavour. Unlike popular Thai dishes, tam kanoon remains relatively unknown outside of the region, and you won't often find it on restaurant menus. It's a true home-style dish, something that reminds me of cozy family meals and the joy of using fresh ingredients straight from our own backyard.

400 g/14 oz. can of young jackfruit, drained
3 tablespoons vegetable oil
200 g/7 oz. pork belly, thinly sliced
1 chicken stock cube, crumbled
300 g/10½ oz. cherry tomatoes, halved
1 tablespoon fish sauce
3 sprigs of coriander/cilantro, chopped
3 spring onions/scallions, chopped
steamed sticky rice or jasmine rice, to serve

CHILLI PASTE
8 dried red chillies/chiles
3 garlic cloves, chopped
1 small shallot, chopped
1 lemongrass stalk, chopped
½ a thumb-sized piece of galangal, sliced
2 teaspoons shrimp paste

SERVES 2–3

First, prepare the chilli paste. In a mortar and pestle or food processor, pound or blend the dried red chillies, garlic, shallot, lemongrass, galangal and shrimp paste to make a smooth paste. Set aside until needed.

Boil the drained young jackfruit in a saucepan of water for 10–15 minutes until tender. Once cooked, drain and shred it into smaller pieces using a fork or your hands.

In a large frying pan/skillet, heat the vegetable oil over a medium heat. Add the chilli paste and sauté for about 2–3 minutes until fragrant. Add the pork belly and cook until the fat renders and the meat has browned.

Crumble in the chicken stock cube and add the cherry tomatoes. Stir well and cook until the tomatoes soften and release their juices.

Add the shredded young jackfruit to the pan and season with fish sauce. Stir everything together and let it cook for a further 5–7 minutes, allowing the flavours to develop.

Turn off the heat and stir in the chopped coriander and spring onions. Serve immediately while hot with steamed sticky rice or jasmine rice.

หมกปลาซาวมอล
MOK PLA SALMON

Salmon wrapped in banana leaves

I loved going to the river near our home to catch small fish when I was a child. It was always exciting to bring them back and help make this dish. We'd mix the fish with a flavourful chilli paste, wrap them in banana leaf parcels, then grill them until the aroma filled the air. It was such a simple yet delicious meal, made even better because it came from our own efforts. Now, I make this dish with salmon instead, but every time I cook it, I'm reminded of those carefree days by the river.

2 large/US extra-large eggs
500 g/1 lb 2 oz. salmon, cut into bite-sized pieces
4 makrut lime leaves, torn
handful of Thai basil leaves
2 large red chillies/chiles, thinly sliced, plus extra to garnish
500 g/1 lb 2 oz. banana leaves (to make parcels)
100 g/3½ oz. kale leaves, cut into bite-sized pieces
steamed rice, to serve
lime wedges, to serve

CHILLI PASTE
10 small dried red chillies/chiles
2 large dried red chillies/chiles
4 garlic cloves, chopped
2 small shallots, chopped
1 teaspoon cumin seeds
1 teaspoon coriander seeds
1 teaspoon salt
2 teaspoons shrimp paste (see page 96)

SERVES 2–3

First, prepare the chilli paste. Boil the dried red chillies in a saucepan with 300 ml/1¼ cups water for 30 minutes, or until softened. Drain the softened chillies. Place the chillies in a blender or mortar and pestle along with the with garlic, shallots, cumin seeds, coriander seeds, salt and shrimp paste. Blend or pound to a smooth paste. Set aside until needed.

In a mixing bowl, combine the chilli paste with the eggs and mix well. Add the salmon pieces, lime leaves, Thai basil leaves and red chillies. Gently toss to coat the salmon evenly.

Lay out the banana leaves and place a few pieces of kale in the centre of each leaf as a base. Spoon the salmon mixture on top of the kale. Add a couple of slices of red chilli as garnish.

Wrap the salmon into parcels by folding the sides of the banana leaves inward and securing them with wooden toothpicks.

Preheat a gas barbecue or charcoal barbecue. Place the banana leaf parcels on the grill and cook over a medium heat for 15–20 minutes, turning occasionally, until the salmon is cooked through and fragrant. Alternatively, you can use a grill/broiler and grill/broil for the same amount of time on a medium heat.

Open the banana leaf parcels, taking care not to scold yourself on any steam. Serve the salmon immediately while hot, either on its own or with steamed rice and with lime wedges for squeezing over.

HUNG LEI CURRY

Pork belly curry

This dish was something of a luxury for us growing up. Traditionally, people would cook it in massive pots – sometimes even larger than a bathtub – during festivals, such as temple fairs, weddings or other big celebrations. It was always a crowd-pleaser. I first tasted this curry at my cousin's wedding celebration, and I immediately fell in love with it. I pestered my grandad to teach me how to make it, and eventually he gave in. I even made it for the MasterChef UK final as part of my Northern Thai banquet. It is served on a *khantoke*, which is a round, low wooden tray or table.

1 kg/2¼ lb. pork belly, cut into 2.5-cm/1-inch cubes
2 tablespoons garam masala
2 tablespoons dark soy sauce
2 tablespoons vegetable oil
1 litre/4 cups chicken or pork stock (no salt)
2 tablespoons fish sauce
120 g/4½ oz. palm sugar (or brown sugar)
80 g/3 oz. tamarind juice (buy this ready-made, see page 118 for a homemade version or use 2½ tablespoons lemon juice)
50 g/1¾ oz. roasted peanuts (see page 47 or use store-bought), plus extra to garnish
thumb-sized piece of fresh ginger, peeled and thinly sliced
100 g/3½ oz. pickled silverskin onions, drained
coriander/cilantro leaves and sliced red chilli/chile, to garnish

CHILLI PASTE
10 large red chillies/chiles, chopped
3 garlic cloves, chopped
1 small shallot, chopped
1 lemongrass stalk, finely chopped
½ a thumb-sized piece of fresh ginger, peeled
2 teaspoons shrimp paste (optional, see page 96)

SERVES 4

Place the pork belly in a bowl and sprinkle over the garam masala and soy sauce, turning the pieces so that they are well coated all over. Cover the bowl with cling film/plastic wrap and transfer to the fridge to marinate for 30 minutes.

Meanwhile, prepare the chilli paste. In a blender or small food processor, combine the red chillies, garlic, shallots, lemongrass, ginger and shrimp paste (if using). Begin blending, adding up to 150 ml/⅔ cup water to make it easier to blend, if needed. Continue blending for a few minutes until it turns into a smooth paste, adjusting the liquid as needed.

Heat the vegetable oil in a wok or medium saucepan over a high heat. Once the wok or pan is hot, add the chilli paste and cook for about 5 minutes to release the aromas.

Add the marinated pork belly and cook, stirring continuously, for 2 minutes until browned. Pour in the chicken stock and stir through.

Season with fish sauce, palm sugar and tamarind juice, then add the roasted peanuts, sliced ginger and pickled onions. Cover the wok or pan with the lid and cook over a low heat for 1 hour, or until the pork belly is tender.

Garnish with coriander leaves, red chilli slices and roughly chopped roasted peanuts. Traditionally, this dish is served with sticky rice, but regular boiled rice is also delicious.

COOKING TIP Use the edge of a teaspoon to peel fresh ginger – it minimizes waste and is safer than using a knife.

Pork in tomato broth
with rice noodles

Every time I cook this dish, it takes me right back to my childhood summers spent at my grandad's barber shop. I would sit there eagerly, waiting for midday when he would close the shop for an hour and take me to our favourite street-food stall. It was the highlight of my summer holidays every year when I visited him. The rich, fragrant broth with its bold flavours, the tender pork and the soft, delicate rice noodles – it was a dish that I could never get enough of. Even now, whenever I prepare this dish, it brings back those cherished memories of sitting in his shop, the smell of haircuts and aftershave lingering in the air, and the excitement of our daily lunch tradition.

3 tablespoons vegetable oil
500 g/1 lb 2 oz. minced/ground pork
500 g/1 lb 2 oz. cherry tomatoes, halved
2 chicken stock cubes, crumbled
3 tablespoons soy bean paste (or white miso paste)
4 tablespoons brown sugar
1 tablespoon tamarind paste
200 g/7 oz. rice noodles, soaked in warm water for 10–15 minutes
handful of beansprouts
2–3 sprigs of coriander/cilantro, chopped
2–3 spring onions/scallions, chopped
lime wedges, to serve

CHILLI PASTE
6 large dried red chillies/chiles, boiled in hot water for 10–15 minutes
6 medium dried red chillies/chiles, boiled in hot water for 10–15 minutes
2 small shallots, chopped
4 garlic cloves, chopped
1 tablespoon shrimp paste
1 lemongrass stalk, chopped
½ a thumb-sized piece of galangal, chopped

SERVES 2–3

First, prepare the chilli paste. In a blender or mortar and pestle, combine the boiled chillies, shallots, garlic, shrimp paste, lemongrass and galangal. Blend or pound to form a smooth paste. Set aside until needed.

Heat the vegetable oil in a large saucepan over a medium heat. Add the chilli paste and stir-fry for 3–4 minutes until fragrant. Add the pork and cook until browned, breaking up any clumps with a wooden spoon.

Stir in the tomatoes and cook for a further 3–5 minutes until they soften and release their juices. Pour in 1 litre/4 cups water, then add the chicken stock cubes, soy bean paste (or miso paste), brown sugar and tamarind paste. Stir well and let the broth simmer for 20–25 minutes, allowing all the flavours to develop.

Meanwhile, bring a separate pan of water to the boil. Add the soaked rice noodles and cook for 2–3 minutes until soft. Drain and set aside.

When ready to serve, divide the noodles between two or three deep bowls and ladle the hot broth over the top. Garnish with beansprouts, chopped coriander and spring onions and serve with lime wedges on the side for added zing.

แกงเห็ดใส่ปลา
GAENG HED SAI PLA

Mushroom curry with smoked mackerel

This dish is one of my mum's all-time favourites. Growing up in the mountains of Northern Thailand, we were surrounded by dense forests full of wild mushrooms, which were a staple in our home cooking. Every morning, local merchants would visit our house, offering foraged mushrooms, and my mum would always buy some to cook for the family. The mushrooms were so fresh and flavourful, it didn't take much to turn them into a delicious dish.

Gaeng hed sai pla is a versatile dish that can be cooked with any type of fish, or you can omit the fish entirely to highlight the earthy richness of the mushrooms. I've recreated this dish using oyster mushrooms that are readily available from local supermarkets – to my delight, it still tastes just as good as it did back home.

1 litre/4 cups chicken or fish stock
200 g/7 oz. oyster mushrooms, torn into bite-sized pieces
200 g/7 oz. smoked mackerel, cut into bite-sized pieces
1 courgette/zucchini, cut into 1-cm/½-inch thick slices
2 tablespoons fish sauce
50 g/1¾ oz. dill, coarsely chopped
steamed sticky rice or jasmine rice, to serve

CHILLI PASTE
4 large hot red chillies/chiles, chopped
4 garlic cloves, chopped
2 small shallots, chopped
2 teaspoons shrimp paste (see page 96)

SERVES 2

First, prepare the chilli paste. In a blender or mortar and pestle, combine the red chillies, garlic, shallots and shrimp paste. Blend or pound to form a smooth paste. Set aside until needed.

In a large saucepan, bring the chicken or fish stock to a gentle boil over a medium heat. Add the chilli paste and stir well, allowing it to dissolve into the broth and the flavours to develop.

Add the mushrooms and smoked mackerel to the pan with the broth. Let it simmer for about 5–7 minutes, allowing the flavours to develop and the mushrooms to soften. Add the courgettes and cook for a further 3–5 minutes, or until tender but still slightly firm. Season the curry with fish sauce, stirring well. Adjust the seasoning to taste.

Turn off the heat and stir in the chopped dill, allowing its aroma to infuse the curry.

Serve the curry immediately while hot with steamed sticky rice or jasmine rice.

PLA NEUNG MANAO

Steamed fish with lime & garlic

This is a dish I vividly remember everyone in Thailand being crazy about. It became trendy, especially among people on low-carb diets. The idea was to skip the rice and pair the tangy, spicy steamed fish with lots of steamed cabbage instead. While I wasn't following the diet, I fell in love with the dish itself – the fresh, tender fish and bold flavours of lime, chilli and garlic were irresistible. Honestly, I could eat this dish every day, diet or not. It's simple, healthy and packed with flavour, making it one of my all-time favourites.

¼ of a white cabbage, very finely shredded
2 x 200-g/7-oz. sea bass fillets (or cod, sea bream or any other white fish fillets)

DRESSING
1 large green chilli/chile, chopped
2 large hot red chillies/chiles, chopped
4 garlic cloves, chopped
4 tablespoons lime juice
4 tablespoons fish sauce
2 tablespoons light soy sauce
1 tablespoon brown sugar
jasmine rice, to serve (optional)

GARNISH
1 lime, cut into wedges
1 large red chilli/chile, cut into long thin slices
coriander/cilantro leaves

steamer

SERVES 2

Place the shredded cabbage on a heatproof plate or tray that fits into a steamer, creating a bed for the fish. Lay the sea bass fillets on top of the cabbage.

Next, prepare the dressing. In a blender or mortar and pestle, combine the green chilli, red chillies, garlic, lime juice, fish sauce, light soy sauce and brown sugar. Blend or pound until smooth.

Drizzle half of the dressing over the sea bass fillets and cabbage, spreading it evenly. Reserve the other half for serving.

Steam the sea bass and cabbage together in a steamer over a medium heat for 10–12 minutes, or until the fish has turned opaque and cooked through and the cabbage is tender.

Carefully transfer the steamed cabbage and sea bass to a serving plate. Pour the remaining dressing over the fish.

Garnish with lime wedges, long thin slices of red chilli and chopped coriander. Perfect paired with jasmine rice and a glass of cold beer.

KHAO MOK GAI

Thai-style chicken biryani

I had never tried *Khao mok gai* until just a couple of years ago when I came across Indian biryani and thought it looked familiar. Curious, I asked my mum about it, and she told me that we have our own Thai version. Excited to learn more, I asked her for the recipe and decided to give it a go. It is quite similar to *Khao mun gai* (see page 23), but with the addition of fragrant dry spices that give it a richer and deeper flavour. It's easy to make, all in one pot and perfect for busy days when you still want something hearty and delicious.

1 tablespoon curry powder
1 teaspoon ground turmeric
½ teaspoon ground cumin
½ teaspoon ground coriander
½ teaspoon salt
1 teaspoon caster/superfine sugar
200 g/1 cup natural/plain yogurt
500 g/1 lb 2 oz. chicken drumsticks
2 tablespoons unsalted butter
200 g/7 oz. jasmine rice, rinsed
1 chicken stock cube, crumbled
1 teaspoon ground cinnamon
3 bay leaves
3 star anise
2 cinnamon sticks

CRISPY SHALLOTS
2 shallots, thinly sliced
1 tablespoon cornflour/cornstarch
200 ml/scant 1 cup vegetable oil

DIPPING SAUCE
7–10 mint leaves, finely chopped
3 sprigs of coriander/cilantro, finely chopped, plus extra leaves to garnish
2 birds eye chillies/chiles, finely chopped
3 garlic cloves, crushed/minced
1 teaspoon salt
3 tablespoons cider vinegar
3 tablespoons caster/superfine sugar

SERVES 2–3

In a large mixing bowl, combine the curry powder, turmeric, cumin, coriander, salt, sugar and yogurt. Add the chicken drumsticks and coat them well in the marinade. Cover with cling film/plastic wrap and leave to marinate in the fridge for at least 1 hour or preferably overnight.

Preheat the oven to 200°C/180°C fan/400°F/Gas 6.

In a large ovenproof casserole dish, melt the butter over a medium heat. Add the marinated chicken drumsticks and sear them on all sides for 5–7 minutes, or until lightly browned. Remove the chicken and set aside.

In the same casserole dish, add the rinsed jasmine rice, crumbled chicken stock cube, ground cinnamon, bay leaves, star anise and cinnamon sticks with 300 ml/1¼ cups water. Stir well to combine.

Nestle the browned chicken drumsticks back into the casserole dish, making sure they are partially submerged in the liquid. Cover with a lid or foil and transfer it to the preheated oven. Bake for 35–40 minutes or until the chicken is fully cooked and the rice is fluffy.

Meanwhile, prepare the crispy shallots. Toss the thinly sliced shallots in the cornflour until lightly coated. Heat the vegetable oil in a small frying pan/skillet over a medium heat. Fry the shallots in the hot oil for 3–4 minutes until golden and crispy. Remove with a slotted spoon and drain on paper towels to absorb any excess oil.

For the dipping sauce, combine the mint, coriander, chillies, garlic, salt, vinegar and sugar in a small bowl. Stir until the sugar is fully dissolved.

Once the chicken and rice are cooked, fluff the rice gently with a fork and remove the whole spices. Serve the fragrant rice and chicken topped with the crispy shallots, garnished with coriander leaves, and the dipping sauce on the side.

Sweet things
ของหวาน

Indulge in the sweet sensation
of Thai desserts and treats.

ชาไทยครีมบลูเล
CHA THAI CREAM BRULEE

Thai milk tea crème brûlée

This is one of the most popular desserts at my restaurant. It's a delightful fusion that combines the silky, creamy texture of classic crème brûlée with the bold, aromatic flavours of Thai milk tea. This dessert is proof that simplicity can lead to incredible results, using just a few ingredients to create something truly special. Let's get started!

450 ml/1¾ cups double/heavy cream
20 g/4 teaspoons Thai tea mix (this can be bought from most Asian stores)
200 g/¾ cup plus 1 tablespoon condensed milk
120 ml/½ cup whole/full-fat milk
5 large/US extra-large egg yolks
4 tablespoons light soft brown sugar

cheesecloth/muslin
4–6 heatproof ramekins (I used small 9-cm/3½-inch ramekins)
deep baking pan
cooks' blowtorch

SERVES 4–6

Preheat the oven to 180°C/160°C fan/250°F/Gas 4.

In a saucepan, heat the cream over a low heat. Sprinkle in the Thai tea mix and stir well. Let it simmer and steep on low heat for about 10 minutes. Strain the mixture using a cheesecloth to remove the tea leaves. Stir in the condensed milk and whole milk, mixing well. Set aside.

In a mixing bowl, lightly beat the egg yolks with a whisk. Gradually pour the Thai tea cream mixture into the yolks while stirring continuously to prevent the eggs from scrambling. Mix until fully combined.

Place the ramekins in a deep baking pan. Slowly pour the cream mixture into the ramekins to avoid spillage. To create a water bath, fill the baking tray with enough boiling water to come halfway up the sides of the ramekins. Cover the pan with foil and bake in the preheated oven for 30–40 minutes (depending on the size of the ramekins).

Check for doneness by gently shaking the ramekins. The edges of the custard should be set and firm, while the centre should have a slight wobble – while hot, the custard may seem like it's not cooked, but does fully set once cooled. Once cooked, remove the cooked custards from the oven and let cool to room temperature before chilling in the fridge for at least 3–4 hours or preferably overnight.

When ready to serve, sprinkle a thin layer of brown sugar evenly over each crème brûlée. Use a cooks' blowtorch to caramelize the sugar until it melts, turns golden and forms a crisp top. Alternatively, place the ramekins under a hot grill/broiler for a few minutes, keeping a close eye to ensure the sugar melts and turns golden without burning. Serve immediately for the perfect contrast of creamy custard and crunchy topping.

พะนาคอตต้ามะลิใส่แยมส้ม
PANNA COTTA MALI SAI SOM

Jasmine panna cotta
with orange & honey compote

I created this dessert for a private dining event with my MasterChef UK family when they were filming near my restaurant. It was such a special day that I even closed the restaurant to host the crew. I wanted to make something unique, inspired by Thai fusion cuisine, and I truly believe the flavours in this dish work together in perfect harmony. The delicate floral aroma of jasmine, the zesty brightness of orange and the natural sweetness of honey blend beautifully, creating a light and elegant dessert that's both refreshing and satisfying.

It was a proud moment for me to serve this dish to my fellow MasterChef UK friends, and their appreciation made it all the more memorable. Now, I'm excited to share it with you!

400 ml/1¾ cup double/heavy cream
150 ml/⅔ cup whole/full-fat milk
60 g/¼ cup caster/superfine sugar
5 jasmine tea bags
3 sheets of gelatine, soaked in water for 10–15 minutes

ORANGE & HONEY COMPOTE
3 large oranges, peeled and segmented
100 g/½ cup caster/superfine sugar
100 g/3½ oz. honey
2 tablespoons lemon juice
grated zest of 1 orange

4–6 serving glasses or moulds

SERVES 4–6

Combine the cream, milk and sugar in a saucepan over a medium heat. Gently stir until the sugar is fully dissolved, ensuring the mixture does not come to the boil.

Add the jasmine tea bags to the cream mixture and steep for 5–7 minutes, allowing the floral flavours to infuse. Remove and discard the tea bags.

Squeeze any excess water from the soaked gelatine sheets and add them to the warm cream mixture. Stir until the gelatine is completely dissolved.

Pour the panna cotta mixture into individual serving glasses or moulds, leave to cool to room temperature, then cover and refrigerate for at least 4–6 hours, or until set.

To make the compote, in a small saucepan, combine the orange segments, sugar, honey, lemon juice and orange zest. Simmer over a low heat for 10–15 minutes, stirring occasionally, until the oranges soften and the mixture thickens slightly. Remove from the heat and leave to cool.

Once the panna cotta is set, spoon the orange and honey compote over the top before serving.

เค๊กสับปะรดใส่มะพร้าว
CAKE SAPPAROD

Pineapple & coconut upside-down cake

This is a recipe I created for a charity event, giving a tropical twist to the classic upside-down cake. It quickly became a crowd-pleaser, with its light texture, balanced sweetness from the coconut and a hint of tanginess from the pineapple. The combination of pineapple and coconut brings a refreshing tropical flavour that is absolutely delicious and perfect for any occasion. It's a dessert that everyone seems to love, and I'm always happy to share it knowing it brings joy to so many.

4 tablespoons melted unsalted butter
100 g/½ cup brown sugar
425 g/14½ oz. canned pineapple slices, drained (but reserve the juice)
13 whole glacé/candied cherries
125 g/½ cup/1⅛ sticks butter
150 g/¾ cup caster/superfine sugar
2 large/US extra-large eggs
225 g/1¾ cups self-raising/rising flour
1 teaspoon baking powder
100 ml/scant ½ cup pineapple juice (reserved from the can)
100 ml/scant ½ cup whole/full-fat milk
100 g/3½ oz. desiccated/shredded coconut
ice cream or custard, to serve (optional)

23-cm/9-inch round cake pan, greased and lined with parchment paper

SERVES 8–10

Preheat the oven to 200°C/180°C fan/400°F/Gas 6.

Pour the melted butter into the prepared cake pan, spreading it evenly across the base. Sprinkle the brown sugar over the butter. Arrange the pineapple slices over the sugar layer, placing one in the centre and the rest in a circle around the edges to cover the base completely. Place a glacé cherry in the centre of each pineapple ring and in between each of the slices around the edge of the pan. Set the pan aside until needed.

In a mixing bowl, cream the butter and caster sugar together until light and fluffy. Add the eggs one at a time, beating well after each addition. Sift in the self-raising flour and baking powder, mixing until just combined. Gradually stir in the pineapple juice, milk and desiccated coconut until the batter is smooth. If there are any canned pineapple slices left over, chop them into small chunks and fold into the batter.

Pour the batter evenly over the prepared pineapple and cherry base in the pan. Bake in the preheated oven for 35–40 minutes, or until a skewer inserted into the centre of the cake comes out clean.

Allow the cake to cool in the pan for 10 minutes. Carefully run a knife around the edges of the pan to loosen the cake, then invert it onto a serving plate. Serve warm or at room temperature with ice cream or custard if liked.

Sticky banoffee pudding

This dessert is my twisted version of two of my all-time favourites – sticky toffee pudding and banoffee pie. I love them and don't see why I should be made to choose between them, so I decided to combine them into one, and the result? An amazing dessert that's indulgent, comforting and absolutely delicious. The rich, sticky sponge infused with caramelized banana flavours, topped with a luscious toffee sauce and finished with a hint of creaminess – it's the perfect balance of textures and flavours. Every time I serve this dessert, whether at my restaurant or to friends and family, it's always a huge hit.

100 g/¾ cup stoned/pitted dates
150 ml/⅔ cup boiling water
2 ripe bananas, mashed
1 teaspoon vanilla extract
175 g/1⅓ cups self-raising/ rising flour
1 teaspoon bicarbonate of/ baking soda
2 large/US extra-large eggs at room temperature
100 g/½ cup/1 stick melted unsalted butter, plus extra for greasing
140 g/¾ cup brown sugar
2 tablespoons black treacle/ molasses
100 ml/scant ½ cup whole/ full-fat milk
whipped cream or ice cream, to serve (optional)

TOFFEE SAUCE
175 g/scant 1 cup brown sugar
225 ml/scant 1 cup double/ heavy cream
1 tablespoon black treacle/ molasses
50 g/3½ tablespoons unsalted butter

20-cm/8-inch square baking dish

SERVES 3–4

Place the dates in a heatproof bowl and pour over the boiling water. Let them soak for 10–15 minutes until softened, then mash with a fork. Set aside until needed.

Preheat the oven to 200°C/180°C fan/400°F/Gas 6 and grease the baking dish with butter.

In a large mixing bowl, combine the mashed bananas, vanilla extract and soaked mashed dates. Stir well to combine.

In a separate bowl, sift together the flour and bicarbonate of soda.

In another bowl, whisk the eggs, melted butter, brown sugar and black treacle until well combined. Slowly add the milk while whisking.

Gradually fold the dry ingredients into the wet mixture, stirring gently until everything is well incorporated and forms a smooth batter.

Pour the batter into the prepared baking dish, levelling the top. Bake in the preheated oven for 30–35 minutes, or until a skewer inserted into the centre comes out clean.

Meanwhile, prepare the toffee sauce. Combine the brown sugar, cream, black treacle and butter in a saucepan over a medium heat. Stir continuously for about 5–7 minutes until the sugar dissolves and the sauce thickens.

Once the pudding is baked, let it cool slightly before drizzling some of the warm toffee sauce over the top, letting it soak into the sponge.

Serve the sticky banoffee pudding warm, topped with extra toffee sauce and a dollop of whipped cream or scoop of vanilla ice cream for an indulgent treat.

ปาท่องโก๋กับสังขยา
PATONGKO KUB SANGKAYA

Thai doughnuts with pandan custard

Patongko are fluffy, golden doughnuts served with a creamy pandan and coconut custard for dipping. They are a snack I could happily eat three times a day. It's such a comforting treat, especially when paired with hot soya milk – dipping the doughnut into the milk before eating is the best part! Back in Thailand, I never thought about making them myself because they were so cheap and easy to buy at the markets. But living in England, I had no choice but to learn how to make them. At first, it seemed complicated, but after making them so many times, I've mastered the process. Now, every batch I make reminds me of those simple joys from home.

DOUGHNUTS

300 g/2¼ cups strong white flour, plus extra for dusting
1 teaspoon instant dried yeast
2 teaspoons baking powder
1 teaspoon bicarbonate of/baking soda
½ teaspoon salt
1 large/US extra-large egg
2 tablespoons melted butter
1 litre/4 cups vegetable oil, for deep frying
caster/superfine sugar, for dusting

PANDAN CUSTARD

3 pandan leaves, cut into 2.5-cm/1-inch pieces (or use 1 teaspoon pandan essence)
300 ml/1¼ cups coconut milk (at least 65% fat content)
3 tablespoons condensed milk
5 tablespoons caster/superfine sugar
1 tablespoon cornflour/cornstarch
3 large/US extra-large egg yolks
4 tablespoons evaporated milk

MAKES 15–20 DOUGHNUTS

First, make the doughnuts. In a mixing bowl, combine the flour, yeast, baking powder, bicarbonate of soda and salt and mix well. Add the egg, melted butter and 130 ml/½ cup water to the dry ingredients. Mix until the dough comes together.

Knead the dough on a floured work surface for 8–10 minutes until it becomes smooth and elastic. Cover the dough with a damp cloth and let it rest for 1–2 hours, or until doubled in size.

Meanwhile, prepare the pandan custard. Blend the pandan leaves with the coconut milk until smooth, then strain through a fine-mesh sieve/strainer to extract the pandan-infused milk. Alternatively, if using pandan essence, mix it directly into the coconut milk.

In a saucepan, whisk together the pandan-infused coconut milk, condensed milk, sugar, cornflour, egg yolks and evaporated milk until fully combined. Cook the mixture over a medium heat, stirring continuously, until it thickens to a custard-like consistency. Remove from heat and set aside to cool.

Roll out the dough on a floured work surface to 1-cm/½-inch thickness. Cut the dough into small rounds, rectangles or your preferred shape.

Heat the vegetable oil in a deep heavy-based pan or deep-fat fryer over a medium heat to 180°C/350°F. Working in batches to avoid overcrowding the pan, fry the doughnuts, turning occasionally, until golden brown and puffed up. This should take about 2–3 minutes per batch. Remove with a slotted spoon, drain on paper towels, then dust with sugar to finish.

Serve the freshly fried doughnuts with the pandan custard on the side for dipping.

Pandan custard tarts

This is my Thai-inspired take on *pastéis de nata*, the classic egg custard tarts I fell in love with during a trip to Portugal. The delicate, creamy custard with its flaky pastry case was unforgettable, and I couldn't help but wonder how to give it a Thai twist. In Thailand, we have pandan custard – a smooth, green custard made with pandan leaves that have a mild, fragrant flavour similar to vanilla but uniquely Thai. I combined these ideas to create this recipe, and the result is a tart that melts in your mouth, with just the right amount of sweetness. It's my way of blending the best of two worlds into one delicious treat.

PANDAN CUSTARD
4 pandan leaves, cut into 2.5-cm/1-inch pieces (or 1½ teaspoons pandan essence)
150 ml/⅔ cup whole/full fat milk
150 ml/⅔ cup condensed milk
150 ml/⅔ cup coconut milk (at least 65% fat content)
4 large/US extra-large eggs
1 tablespoon cornflour/cornstarch

PASTRY DOUGH
260 g/2 cups plain/all-purpose flour
4 tablespoons caster/superfine sugar
150 g/⅔ cup/1¼ sticks softened unsalted butter
2 large/US extra-large egg yolks
2 teaspoons vanilla extract

TO SERVE
whipped cream (optional)
10-cm/4-inch cutter or glass rim
10–12 individual 7.5-cm/3-inch tart moulds (or use a 12-hole muffin pan)

MAKES 10–12 TARTS

First, prepare the pastry. In a mixing bowl, combine the flour and sugar. Add the softened butter and mix until the texture resembles breadcrumbs. Add the egg yolks and vanilla extract, mixing until the dough comes together. Form the dough into a ball, wrap it in cling film/plastic wrap and refrigerate for at least 30 minutes.

Meanwhile, make the custard. Blend the pandan leaves with the milk until smooth, then strain through a fine-mesh sieve/strainer to extract the pandan-infused milk. Alternatively, if using pandan essence, mix it directly into the milk.

In a mixing bowl, combine the pandan-infused milk, condensed milk, coconut milk, eggs and cornflour. Whisk until combined, then set aside.

Preheat the oven to 200°C/180°C fan/400°F/Gas 6.

Roll out the dough on a floured work surface to 3-mm/⅛-inch thickness. Using the cookie cutter or glass rim, punch out discs of dough. Press the discs into the tart moulds. Trim away any excess pastry around the rims for a neat finish.

Prick the base of the pastry cases with a fork, then line with parchment paper and fill with baking weights or dried beans. Bake in the preheated oven for 10–12 minutes, remove the weights and paper, then bake for a further 5 minutes until lightly golden.

Carefully pour the pandan custard into the baked tart shells, filling them nearly to the top. Lower the oven temperature to 190°C/170°C fan/375°F/Gas 5 and bake the filled tarts for 15–20 minutes, or until the custard is just set but still slightly jiggly in the centre. Let the tarts cool completely in the moulds before removing them. Serve the tarts at room temperature, either on their own or with whipped cream.

เอแคร์ใส้ครีมสังขยา
SANGKAYA ÉCLAIR

Éclairs with pandan cream

Pandan, also known as screw pine, is a fragrant leaf commonly used in south-east Asian cuisine, known for its vibrant green colour and distinctive flavour. I created this dish while preparing for MasterChef UK It's a perfect fusion of Thai flavours and French technique. Although I didn't get the chance to use it during the competition, I'm excited to share this recipe now. It's light, fragrant and absolutely delicious – perfect for anyone who loves a little twist on tradition.

PANDAN CUSTARD
- 4 pandan leaves, cut into 2.5-cm/1-inch pieces (or 1½ teaspoons pandan essence)
- 150 ml/⅔ cup whole/full fat milk
- 150 ml/⅔ cup condensed milk
- 150 ml/⅔ cup coconut milk (at least 65% fat content)
- 4 large/US extra-large eggs
- 2 tablespoons cornflour/cornstarch
- 200 ml/scant 1 cup double/heavy cream, whipped to stiff peaks

CHOUX PASTRY DOUGH
- 100 g/½ cup/1 stick unsalted butter
- 150 g/generous 1 cup plain/all-purpose flour
- 4 large/US extra-large eggs

TO DECORATE (OPTIONAL)
- melted dark/bittersweet chocolate, to decorate (optional)

baking sheet lined with parchment paper
piping/pastry bag fitted with a wide nozzle

MAKES 8–10 ECLAIRS

Make the pandan custard following the instructions on page 164. Once cooled, gently fold the custard into the whipped cream to create a light and creamy pandan filling. Cover and refrigerate until needed.

Preheat the oven to 220°C/200°C fan/425°F/Gas 7.

Next, make the choux pastry dough. In a saucepan, combine the water butter and 250 ml/1 cup water. Heat over a medium heat until the butter melts and the mixture come to a boil. Remove from the heat and immediately stir in the flour. Mix vigorously until the dough comes together and pulls away from the sides of the pan. Return the pan to a low heat and cook the dough for 1–2 minutes, stirring continuously, to dry it out slightly.

Transfer the dough to a mixing bowl and let it cool for 5–10 minutes. Using a wooden spoon or electric hand mixer, gradually beat in the eggs, one at a time, mixing well after each addition, until the dough is smooth and glossy. Transfer the choux pastry dough to the piping bag. Pipe lines of the dough onto the prepared baking sheet, about 8–10 cm/3–4 inches along, spacing them apart to allow for expansion.

Bake in the preheated oven for 20–25 minutes, or until puffed and golden brown. Turn off the oven, leave the door slightly ajar and let the éclairs dry out for 10 minutes. Cool completely on a wire rack.

Split the eclairs lengthways or poke a small hole in both ends to fill, then pipe the chilled pandan cream into the éclairs until generously filled. Glaze the top of the éclairs with melted chocolate for extra decoration if preferred. Serve the éclairs fresh on the day they are made.

KHAO NIAO MAMUANG

Classic mango sticky rice
in coconut milk

This is one of my all-time favourite desserts – I could eat it every day! It's not overly sweet, with a lovely balance of creamy, sweet and slightly tangy flavours from the mango. While you can use any ripe mango for this dish, the best option is the honey gold mango from Thailand. That said, it's not always easy to find, so use whatever is available.

In this recipe, I'll teach you a simple trick for cooking sticky rice in the microwave, without needing to soak it overnight. It gives you the perfect texture for this classic dessert.

200 g/7 oz. sticky rice
500 ml/2 cups boiling water
400 ml/1⅔ cups coconut milk (at least 65% fat content)
80 g/⅓ cup palm sugar (or brown sugar)
¼ teaspoon salt
1 teaspoon cornflour/cornstarch
1 large ripe mango, peeled and cut into bite-sized pieces

SERVES 2

In a microwave-safe bowl with a lid, add the sticky rice and pour in the boiling water. Stir well with a fork to ensure the water completely covers the rice and let it sit for 10 minutes.

After soaking, rinse the rice 2–3 times in a sieve/strainer under cold running water until the water runs clear. Return the rice to the microwave-safe bowl. Add an equal amount of water – the water level should be even with the rice, just touching the surface, but not completely covering it. Cover the bowl with the lid, leaving a small gap for steam to escape.

Microwave on high for 7 minutes. Stir the rice, then microwave for a further 5 minutes. Stir again and check for doneness. If the rice is still undercooked, add 1–2 tablespoons water and microwave in 1-minute intervals until the rice is soft. Keep the bowl covered and set aside.

In a small saucepan, heat 300 ml/1¼ cups of the coconut milk over a low heat and stir in 60 g/generous ¼ cup of the sugar. Simmer for a few minutes until the sugar dissolves. Pour the mixture over the cooked sticky rice, stirring well to combine. Let it rest for 10 minutes to absorb the flavours.

In the same saucepan, heat the remaining coconut milk over a low heat. Add the remaining sugar and the salt and cornflour, stirring until the sauce thickens slightly. This is the coconut sauce for drizzling.

When ready to serve, pile the sticky coconut rice in mounds on individual serving plates. Arrange the chopped mango alongside the rice and drizzle over the coconut sauce.

คาราเมลมะพร้าวพุดดิ้ง
CARAMEL MAPROW PUDDING

Coconut caramel pudding

Coconut caramel pudding, also known as coconut flan or coconut caramel custard, is a popular sweet treat in Thai cuisine and other Asian cuisines. The first time I had this dessert was during my time in Japan, and I fell in love with it instantly. The silky, smooth texture and rich caramel flavour were simply irresistible. But of course, I couldn't resist putting my own Thai twist on it!

I decided to recreate this dish by adding coconut, and it turned out to be even better than the original. The subtle tropical notes from the coconut blend perfectly with the creamy pudding and sweet caramel, making it a dessert that feels both familiar and exotic at the same time.

115 g/½ cup plus 1¼ tablespoons caster/superfine sugar
300 ml/1¼ cups coconut milk (at least 65% fat content)
2 eggs, at room temperature and beaten
1 teaspoon vanilla essence
toasted desiccated/shredded coconut, to decorate (optional)

4 individual pudding moulds or ramekins
deep baking pan

SERVES 4

Place 3 tablespoons of the sugar in a small saucepan with 1½ tablespoons water and set over a medium heat. Let it cook without stirring for about 3–5 minutes until the sugar dissolves and turns into a golden caramel. Gently swirl the pan, if needed, but do not stir. Carefully pour the caramel into the pudding moulds or ramekins, tilting them slightly to evenly coat the base. Set aside to cool and harden.

Preheat the oven to 180°C/160°C fan/350°F/Gas 4.

In a bowl, whisk together the coconut milk, remaining sugar, beaten eggs and vanilla essence until well combined and smooth. Strain the mixture through a fine-mesh sieve/strainer to remove any lumps and achieve a silky texture.

Place the pudding moulds in a deep baking pan. Slowly pour the custard mixture into the moulds over the caramel to avoid spillage. To create a water bath, fill the baking pan with enough boiling water to come halfway up the sides of the moulds. Cover the tray with foil and bake in the preheated oven for 30–40 minutes, or until the pudding is set but still slightly wobbly in the centre. Remove the puddings from the oven and let cool to room temperature. Once cool, refrigerate for at least 3–4 hours, or until fully chilled.

When ready to serve, run a knife around the edge of each pudding and gently invert onto a plate, letting the caramel sauce drizzle down over the pudding. Decorate the plates by scattering over a little toasted desiccated coconut, if you like.

Index

A
aubergine/eggplant with tofu, stir-fried 122

B
bacon: bubble & squeak spring rolls 51
banana leaves, salmon wrapped in 143
bananas: sticky banoffee pudding 163
beef: beef & pineapple curry 96
   crying tiger beef salad 67
   spicy beef broth with rice noodles 78
   Thai grilled beef meatballs 48
biryani, Thai-style chicken 152
bread: crispy pork & prawn toasts 44
broths *see* soups & broths
bubble & squeak spring rolls 51
burgers, Chinese chicken 32–4
burritos, Thai chicken salad 41
butternut squash: Northern Thai pumpkin curry 111
   spiced butternut squash fritters 55

C
cabbage: bubble & squeak spring rolls 51
   spicy Asian-style salad 32–4
cake, pineapple & coconut upside-down 160
caramel: coconut caramel pudding 172
chicken: chicken noodle curry 92
   chicken satay 24
   Chinese chicken burger 32–4
   crispy garlic chicken wings 38
   drunken noodles 126
   Hainanese chicken rice 23
   herbal broth with chicken 139
   Japanese stir-fried wheat noodles with a Thai twist & yakisoba sauce 121
   rice soup 81
   spicy Asian-style salad 32–4
   spicy coconut broth with chicken 74
   stir-fried chicken with holy basil 114
   Thai chicken noodle soup 86
   Thai chicken salad burritos 41
   Thai green chicken curry 99
   Thai-style chicken biryani 152
chillies/chiles 10
   chilli & lime dipping sauce 64
   herbal broth with chicken 139
   jackfruit Thai curry 107
   Northern Thai larb 132
   Northern Thai pork chilli dip 135
   rice noodles with fish curry sauce 20
   sweet chilli sauce 51
   Thai fish cakes 19
   young jackfruit salad 140
Chinese chicken burger with spicy Asian-style salad 32–4
choux pastry: éclairs with pandan cream 168
coconut: pineapple & coconut upside-down cake 160
coconut milk 10
   beef & pineapple curry 96
   chicken noodle curry 92
   chicken satay 24
   classic mango sticky rice in coconut milk 171
   coconut caramel pudding 172
   duck leg confit with red curry 108
   Massaman lamb curry 95
   pandan custard 164
   spicy coconut broth with chicken 74
   steamed seafood curry 136
   Thai green chicken curry 99
compote, orange & honey 159
condensed milk: pandan custard tarts 167
   Thai milk tea crème brûlée 156
crab: chunky crab omelette with spicy fish sauce 31
   yellow curry stir-fry 129
cream: éclairs with pandan cream 168
   jasmine panna cotta 159
   sticky banoffee pudding 163
   Thai milk tea crème brûlée 156
crème brûlée, Thai milk tea 156
crispy garlic chicken wings 38
crispy pork & prawn toasts 44
crispy prawn & lemongrass wontons 60
crying tiger beef salad 67
curry 90–111
   beef & pineapple curry 96
   chicken noodle curry 92
   duck leg confit with red curry 108
   jackfruit Thai curry 107
   Massaman lamb curry 95
   mixed seafood sour curry 103
   mushroom curry with smoked mackerel 148
   Northern Thai pumpkin curry 111
   pork belly curry 144
   rice noodles with fish curry sauce 20
   salmon jungle curry 100
   sour curry soup 89
   steamed seafood curry 136
   Thai green chicken curry 99
   Thai-style chicken biryani 152
   vegetable jungle curry 104
   yellow curry stir-fry 129
custard, pandan 164
   pandan custard tarts 167

D
dates: sticky banoffee pudding 163
dips: chilli & lime dipping sauce 64
   lime yogurt dip 55
   Northern Thai pork chilli dip 135
   spicy peanut dipping sauce 41
   sweet chilli sauce 51
doughnuts, Thai 164
drunken noodles 126
duck leg confit with red curry 108
dumplings, pork 56

E
éclairs with pandan cream 168
eggs: chunky crab omelette 31
   classic pad Thai 118
   sai ua scotch eggs 52
   Thai milk tea crème brûlée 156
   Thai-style mussel pancake 28

F
fish: mushroom curry with smoked mackerel 148
   rice noodles with fish curry sauce 20
   salmon jungle curry 100
   salmon wrapped in banana leaves 143
   sour curry soup 89
   steamed fish with lime & garlic 151
   Thai fish cakes 19
fish sauce 10
   chunky crab omelette with spicy fish sauce 31
fritters, spiced butternut squash 55

G
garlic: crispy garlic chicken wings 38
   Northern Thai larb 132

rice soup 81
steamed fish with lime & garlic 151
gravy sauce, stir-fried rice noodles with 125

H
Hainanese chicken rice 23
herbal broth with chicken 139
honey: orange & honey compote 159

J
jackfruit: jackfruit Thai curry 107
young jackfruit salad 140
Japanese stir-fried wheat noodles with a Thai twist & yakisoba sauce 121
jasmine panna cotta with orange & honey compote 159
jungle curry: salmon jungle curry 100
vegetable jungle curry 104

L
lamb: Massaman lamb curry 95
larb, Northern Thai 132
lemongrass 9
crispy prawn & lemongrass wontons 60
lettuce: crying tiger beef salad 67
limes 9
chilli & lime dipping sauce 64
lime yogurt dip 55
steamed fish with lime & garlic 151

M
mackerel, mushroom curry with smoked 148
mango sticky rice in coconut milk 171
Massaman lamb curry 95
meatballs, Thai grilled beef 48
mushroom curry with smoked mackerel 148

mussels: Thai-style mussel pancake 28

N
noodles 10
chicken noodle curry 92
classic pad Thai with king prawns 118
drunken noodles 126
Japanese stir-fried wheat noodles with a Thai twist & yakisoba sauce 121
mixed seafood clear soup 85
mixed seafood salad 27
rice noodles with fish curry sauce 20
rice noodles with tomato-based broth & pork 147
spicy beef broth with rice noodles 78
stir-fried rice noodles with gravy sauce 125
Thai chicken noodle soup 86
Thai-style suki yaki with tofu 82
Northern Thai larb 132
Northern Thai pork chilli dip 135
Northern Thai pumpkin curry 111

O
omelettes: chunky crab omelette with spicy fish sauce 31
Thai-style mussel pancake 28
orange & honey compote 159

P
pad Thai: classic pad Thai with king prawns 118
pandan custard: éclairs with pandan cream 168
pandan custard tarts 167
Thai doughnuts with pandan custard 164
panna cotta, jasmine 159
peanut butter: chicken satay 24

spicy peanut dipping sauce 41
peanuts 10
pork belly curry 144
pineapple: beef & pineapple curry 96
pineapple & coconut upside-down cake 160
pork: crispy pork & prawn toasts 44
grilled pork skewer 16
jackfruit Thai curry 107
Northern Thai larb 132
Northern Thai pork chilli dip 135
pork belly curry 144
pork dumplings 56
rice noodles with tomato-based broth & pork 147
sai ua scotch eggs 52
stir-fried rice noodles with gravy sauce 125
tangy & spicy pork broth 75
Thai steamed buns 35
young jackfruit salad 140
potatoes: bubble & squeak spring rolls 51
prawns/shrimp: classic pad Thai with king prawns 118
crispy pork & prawn toasts 44
crispy prawn & lemongrass wontons 60
Thai fish cakes 19
Thai hot & sour soup with prawns 70

R
rice: classic mango sticky rice in coconut milk 171
Hainanese chicken rice 23
rice soup 81
Thai-style chicken biryani 152

S
sai ua scotch eggs 52
salads: crying tiger beef salad 67
mixed seafood salad 27
spicy Asian-style salad 32-4

Thai chicken salad burritos 41
Thai swede salad 47
watermelon salad with Thai basil & mint 61
young jackfruit salad 140
salmon: salmon jungle curry 100
salmon wrapped in banana leaves 143
sour curry soup 89
satay, chicken 24
scotch eggs, sai ua 52
seafood: mixed seafood clear soup 85
mixed seafood salad 27
mixed seafood sour curry 103
steamed seafood curry 136
stir-fried mixed seafood 117
see also mussels; squid, etc
shallots: crispy shallots 152
Northern Thai larb 132
skewers: chicken satay 24
grilled pork skewer 16
smoked mackerel, mushroom curry with 148
soups & broths 68-89
herbal broth with chicken 139
mixed seafood clear soup 85
rice noodles with tomato-based broth & pork 147
rice soup 81
sour curry soup 89
spicy beef broth with rice noodles 78
spicy coconut broth with chicken 74
tangy & spicy pork broth 75
Thai chicken noodle soup 86
Thai hot & sour soup with prawns 70
Thai-style suki yaki with tofu 82
sour curry soup 89
spiced butternut squash fritters 55

Thank you

spicy Asian-style salad 32–4
spicy beef broth with rice noodles 78
spicy coconut broth with chicken 74
spicy peanut dipping sauce 41
spring rolls, bubble & squeak 51
squash: Northern Thai pumpkin curry 111
  spiced butternut squash fritters 55
squid: grilled squid with chilli & lime dipping sauce 64
steamed buns, Thai 35
sticky banoffee pudding 163
stir-fries 112–29
  classic pad Thai with king prawns 118
  drunken noodles 126
  Japanese stir-fried wheat noodles with a Thai twist & yakisoba sauce 121
  stir-fried aubergine with tofu 122
  stir-fried chicken with holy basil 114
  stir-fried mixed seafood 117
  stir-fried rice noodles with gravy sauce 125
  yellow curry stir-fry 129
suki yaki: Thai-style suki yaki with tofu 82
swede: Thai swede salad 47
sweet chilli sauce 51

T
tamarind 10
  pork belly curry 144
tangy & spicy pork broth 75
tarts, pandan custard 167
Thai basil 9
  watermelon salad with Thai basil & mint 61
Thai chicken noodle soup 86
Thai chicken salad burritos 41

Thai doughnuts with pandan custard 164
Thai fish cakes 19
Thai green chicken curry 99
Thai grilled beef meatballs 48
Thai hot & sour soup with prawns 70
Thai milk tea crème brûlée 156
Thai steamed buns 35
Thai-style chicken biryani 152
Thai-style mussel pancake 28
Thai-style suki yaki with tofu 82
Thai swede salad 47
toffee: sticky banoffee pudding 163
tofu: mixed seafood clear soup 85
  stir-fried aubergine with tofu 122
  Thai-style suki yaki with tofu 82
tomatoes: rice noodles with tomato-based broth & pork 147

V
vegetables: vegetable jungle curry 104
  see also individual types of vegetable

W
watermelon salad 61
wonton wrappers: crispy prawn & lemongrass wontons 60
  pork dumplings 56

Y
yakisoba sauce, Japanese stir-fried wheat noodles with 121
yellow curry stir-fry 129
yogurt: lime yogurt dip 55

This book means a lot to me, so I want to take a moment to say thank you to the people who have made it possible.

First, my biggest thank you goes to my **grandad**. He was the first person who taught me how to cook. I still remember standing next to him, watching him work his magic in the kitchen. He never used recipes, just cooked from his heart, and I learned to do the same. His food was always full of love, and that's something I've carried with me my whole life. I hope he would be proud of me today.

To my **mom and aunties**, thank you for showing me the power of food. I grew up watching you cook, learning your tricks and feeling the love in every meal. You taught me that food is more than just eating – it's about sharing and taking care of people.

To my **brother**, I miss you every day. There are dishes in this book that I cooked because you loved them so much. Every time I make them, I think of us as kids, sitting together, laughing and enjoying food. Cooking these dishes brings back those happy memories, and I hope that through this book, a little piece of you stays with me forever.

To my **fiancé**, my **friends**, my **team at the restaurant**, **Anne (AK Artistmanagement)** and everyone at **RPS** who has supported me – thank you for believing in me. You've been there through all the crazy ideas, the late nights and the hard times, and I couldn't have done this without you.

And finally, thank you to **you**, the reader of this book. Whether you are an experienced cook or just starting out, I hope you enjoy these recipes as much as I have. Cooking is not only about making food, it's about sharing, about bringing people together and about creating memories. I hope this book helps you to do just that.

With all my heart,

Chariya